An Activity Book

Bloodthirsty & Bewitched

For Strange & Unusual Adults

Written by Meredith Erin
Illustrated by Matt Snow

ISBN: 978-1-7365435-4-2
Library of Congress Cataloging-in-Publication Data
is available for this title.

Originally published in softcover by Boredwalk in 2024

Written by Meredith Erin and Matt Snow
Editing by Matt Snow
Proofreading by Matt Snow
Cover design, layout, and illustrations
by Matt Snow for Boredwalk
Printed in Canada

Boredwalk
9120 Norwalk Blvd
Santa Fe Springs CA 90670
www.boredwalk.com

Welcome ghoulish f(r)iend! Grab your most opulent candelabra, your favorite writing & drawing implements, and settle in for some old fashioned whimsy as we invite you into our papery parlor.

Within this inky tome you will find countless* pages full of darkly droll diversions designed to delight and distract you from the intolerably bright outside world.

**(OK, it's 96 pages, but we're setting a mood here!)*

Crossword puzzles, word searches, logic puzzles, coloring pages, math puzzles, creative writing prompts, mazes, matching games, and so many more activities will be found in the following pages. Each activity is perfect for keeping your mind as sharp as your fangs. Some of these amusements are ideal for solo sport, while others are best reserved for the next time you gather with your sirens, coven, wolfpack, etc. Truly, it is fun for the entire supernatural family!

NOTA BENE: This activity book was written & illustrated for entertainment purposes and is not based on any specific belief system, grimoire, or religious practice. Please do not contact us to complain about what we got wrong about vampires or the Devil; all of this stuff is made up, anyway.

So strap in, you dreadful denizen of this dreary world — amusement awaits!

WORD SEARCH

PARAPSYCHOLOGY

LIKE REAL PSYCHOLOGY, BUT BETTER!

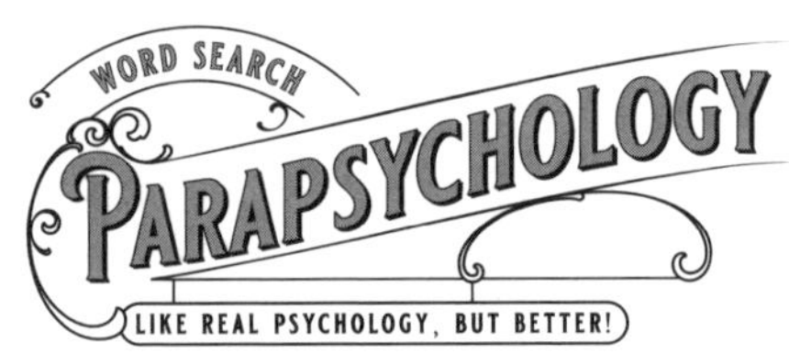

You don't have to be psychic to perceive the paranormal phenomena in this puzzle — all you need is a keen eye and an inquisitive streak!

V	W	P	Q	T	J	F	K	T	F	P	P	Y	A	N	C	O	K	T	K	C	H	U	D	B	S	F	G	R	F
Y	T	X	V	E	A	C	J	S	V	R	Q	Y	S	E	D	I	V	I	N	A	T	I	O	N	J	V	E	G	Q
I	Z	R	M	L	V	V	Y	C	G	E	V	K	T	H	M	L	U	W	V	B	F	D	M	K	Z	A	U	U	L
J	H	M	O	E	V	M	L	R	I	C	E	A	R	S	Y	A	T	N	C	Q	X	K	G	X	T	T	F	X	S
A	H	D	C	K	Q	S	P	Y	U	O	X	K	A	Y	H	D	X	B	M	E	U	E	H	B	V	F	S	A	J
Q	G	C	D	I	R	D	A	I	B	G	U	N	L	X	Q	A	R	J	G	C	I	I	N	R	P	D	Y	X	T
Z	S	X	N	N	E	J	R	N	O	N	M	W	P	S	G	H	P	O	M	V	J	C	A	D	S	K	Z	Z	R
Z	L	O	S	E	Q	S	A	G	D	I	P	Z	R	E	E	Y	J	E	K	R	X	Z	W	H	Y	L	Q	Z	B
F	D	J	U	S	Z	N	P	O	Y	T	Y	A	O	E	X	P	Q	R	S	I	U	O	D	G	C	M	A	Q	H
X	I	L	M	I	J	Z	S	C	A	I	W	R	J	R	T	N	Y	A	T	H	N	T	M	Z	H	W	H	J	P
T	Q	A	M	S	F	W	Y	B	H	O	P	O	E	A	R	O	G	F	E	E	I	E	K	A	I	F	R	X	J
O	X	E	O	H	I	L	C	S	O	N	O	C	C	N	A	S	P	J	L	K	V	F	T	N	C	U	Y	I	L
D	N	H	N	Q	P	V	H	S	W	Z	P	C	T	S	S	I	Z	J	E	J	R	L	T	I	Z	R	T	U	A
T	I	Y	I	L	U	T	O	X	H	Q	Z	W	I	N	E	S	S	C	P	M	R	T	L	I	C	O	P	B	S
X	L	K	N	L	G	Z	L	O	U	Q	R	B	O	B	N	J	C	M	A	S	K	S	G	T	N	B	O	F	Y
Y	O	U	G	L	T	F	O	F	G	D	J	H	N	R	S	S	B	G	T	I	X	E	T	T	R	G	S	F	U
E	Q	S	C	D	J	U	G	P	E	B	G	F	Y	D	O	I	S	J	H	S	Q	Q	X	O	K	H	S	O	H
L	L	R	M	I	U	D	Y	U	D	T	C	X	X	B	R	X	U	Y	Y	K	D	C	M	Y	I	Q	E	N	O
E	P	U	I	G	D	Z	H	E	A	L	I	N	G	F	Y	L	G	E	A	Q	Q	L	S	R	D	O	S	C	A
B	F	W	N	T	B	D	N	H	S	E	N	R	A	W	P	D	P	I	I	T	U	A	B	P	Y	N	S	H	W
X	T	N	D	E	A	M	R	O	R	A	P	W	U	B	E	T	E	K	D	N	R	I	T	R	U	T	I	C	I
Y	X	H	C	L	Z	M	G	E	U	K	C	W	Z	Z	R	G	N	A	X	R	F	R	G	N	A	H	O	M	M
D	A	S	O	E	L	B	P	Q	A	K	J	R	I	K	C	V	N	I	I	M	T	V	R	U	H	W	N	E	K
X	P	I	N	P	E	V	V	R	N	M	D	O	F	C	E	A	F	P	H	E	N	O	M	E	N	A	X	D	L
Q	N	G	T	O	V	O	Z	P	D	F	I	Z	J	V	P	P	U	N	V	R	M	Y	O	P	T	F	T	I	H
A	L	E	R	R	I	D	N	D	I	J	C	N	H	K	T	I	A	B	G	I	U	A	O	V	I	Q	T	U	U
H	T	A	O	T	T	U	P	V	G	B	W	S	G	M	I	N	L	R	E	A	Y	N	T	D	X	Z	Y	M	P
T	X	Z	L	J	A	W	Y	G	G	B	O	I	D	A	O	V	U	W	V	H	J	T	P	C	C	L	R	R	D
L	V	N	J	C	T	X	W	L	P	Y	M	E	B	A	N	F	V	J	V	M	Z	D	S	F	B	B	M	P	Y
O	B	C	Z	E	E	K	U	H	O	A	D	P	Y	R	O	K	I	N	E	T	I	C	R	N	K	A	V	P	P

extrasensory perception
psychic
medium
seer
telekinesis
mind control

pyrokinetic
telepathy
parapsychology
astral projection
clairvoyant
shapeshifting

teleport
precognition
levitate
hydrokinetic
hypnosis
phenomena

divination
scrying
lucid dreaming
possession
healing
summoning

HAIKU

Haunted Castle

3 LINES, 17 SYLLABLES, COUNTLESS SPIRITS

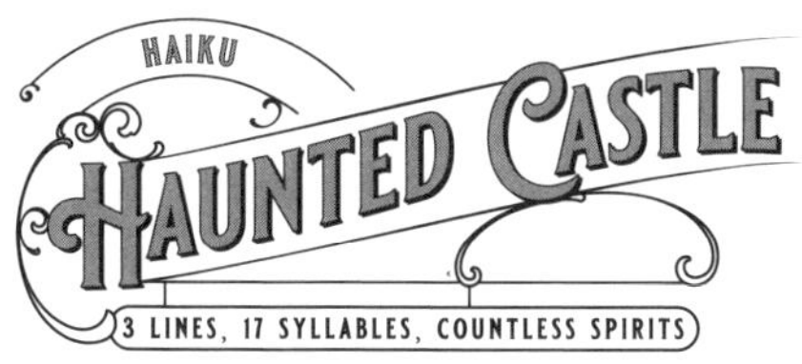

Is a castle really a castle if it isn't teeming with ghosts, phantoms, wraiths, poltergeists, and other unwelcoming incorporeal apparitions? We say thee nay! Compose a haiku about a haunted castle on the lines below.

Tip: Haiku is a Japanese poetic form comprised of three lines. The first line has five syllables, the second line has seven syllables, and the last line has five syllables.

____

____

____

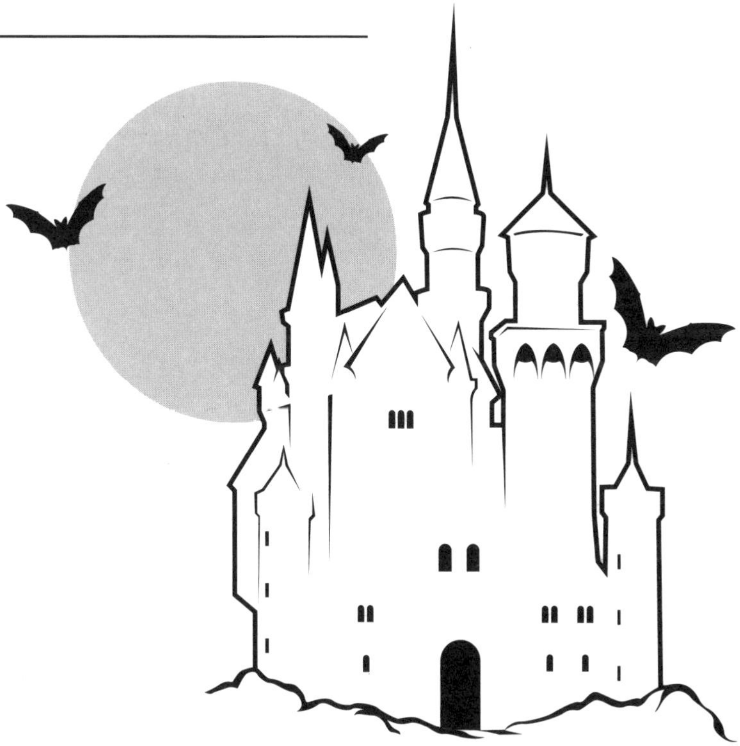

Solve the puzzle below to discover how many ghosts are haunting the abandoned castle!

× =

− =

÷ 2 = 45

45 ÷ (÷ 2) =

\+ (+) = ?

MAIN
VILLAIN
ENERGY

Fill in the blanks below with the missing word or phrase. Then plug those words into the corresponding blanks on the next page to complete the story. *(Note: You can do this one alone, but it's also fun to do with a sleep paralysis demon!)*

1. Adjective ____________________
2. Famous last name ____________________
3. Place ____________________
4. Famous woman ____________________
5. Transport vessel ____________________
6. Adjective ____________________
7. Noun ____________________
8. Era (time period) ____________________
9. Noun ____________________
10. Plural noun ____________________
11. Plural noun ____________________
12. Celebrity ____________________
13. Adjective ____________________
14. Adjective ____________________
15. Noun ____________________
16. Celebrity ____________________
17. Adjective ____________________
18. Adjective ____________________
19. Adjective ____________________

PREPOSTEROUSLY WEALTHY FAMILY FOUND SLAIN IN ANCESTRAL HOME; SKULLDUGGERY SUSPECTED

Authorities are shocked by a ________________ scene uncovered at the ________________ family estate in ________________ this morning. The family's matriarch, ________________, was found chopped into pieces and stuffed into a(n) ________________ in the driveway. Other family members were the apparent victims of a stabbing, in what police are describing as a particularly ________________ end.

The family made their fortune in ________________ in the __________, but in recent years has become known for ____________________. The family amassed tens of million dollars in additional wealth, selling ______________ to ____________. There is now speculation that this crime may have been motivated by revenge.

Police chief ______________ told reporters at a press conference today that the ______________ killings will be investigated until the culprit is brought to justice. There are no suspects at this time, but police are hoping that a(n) ___________ ______________ with more information may have a lead.

Close friend of the family ________________ issued a statement saying "whoever committed this ________________ crime must answer for what they have done. I am shocked that such a ______________ thing could happen to such a ________________ family."

If you know a lot about the supernatural you might have a ghost of a chance with this puzzle!

ACROSS:

3. New York village with a headless horseman problem

5. Ghostly apparition of Irish folklore believed to predict death

7. She'll come to the mirror if you call her name three times

9. Social network with a ghostly mascot

11. Board used as a medium for contacting spirits

12. Abandoned island prison rumored to be haunted

16. She haunts the 2nd floor ladies restroom at Hogwarts

17. Blinky, Pinky, Inky, and Clyde's target

18. Ghostly trucker who appears in *Pee-Wee's Big Adventure*

20. Ghostly slang term for a government assassin

23. Firearm manufacturing heiress who insisted on endless construction at her home to keep ghosts at bay

25. Wes Craven's pun-loving haunter of teenage dreams

26. House haunted by the spirit of Abraham Lincoln

27. The friendly ghost

DOWN:

1. *The Haunting of Hill House* author

2. General Mills' haunted breakfast cereal

4. Freelance bio-exorcist

6. Classic horror film franchise whose main antagonist is known as "The Tall Man"

8. "I see ________ people."

10. Classic horror film franchise whose ghosts are announced with the iconic line "They're here."

13. Ghost ship that inspired *The Pirates of the Caribbean*

14. Mexican holiday for paying respects to the dead

15. "Weeping Woman" ghost eternally cursed to search for her children

19. Haunted hotel in *The Shining*

20. Dickens character who is visited by three ghosts

21. Haunted house built on the site of San Diego's first public gallows

22. A derivative of the French word for "session"

24. Viscous residue left behind by spirits

1
2
3
4
5
6
7
8
9
10
11
12
13
14
15
16
17
18
19
20
21
22
23
24
25
26
27

SPOT THE DIFFERENCE

HAUNTED HOUSE

SHARP-EYED SHENANIGANS!

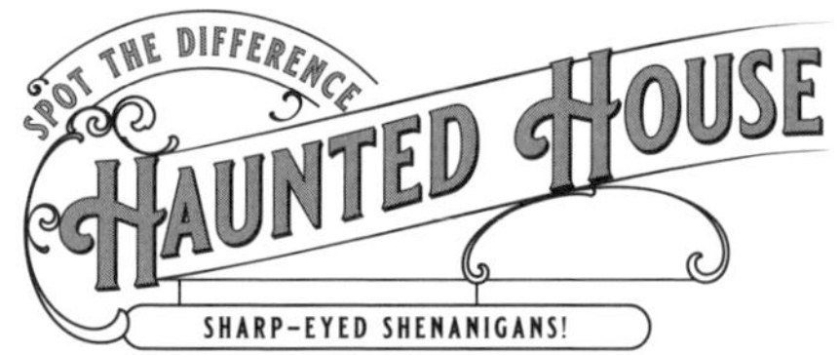

The illustrations below and on the next page may *look* the same, but they actually contain slight differences. See if you can spot all ten of the objects that are either missing or different from those in the illustration on the next page!

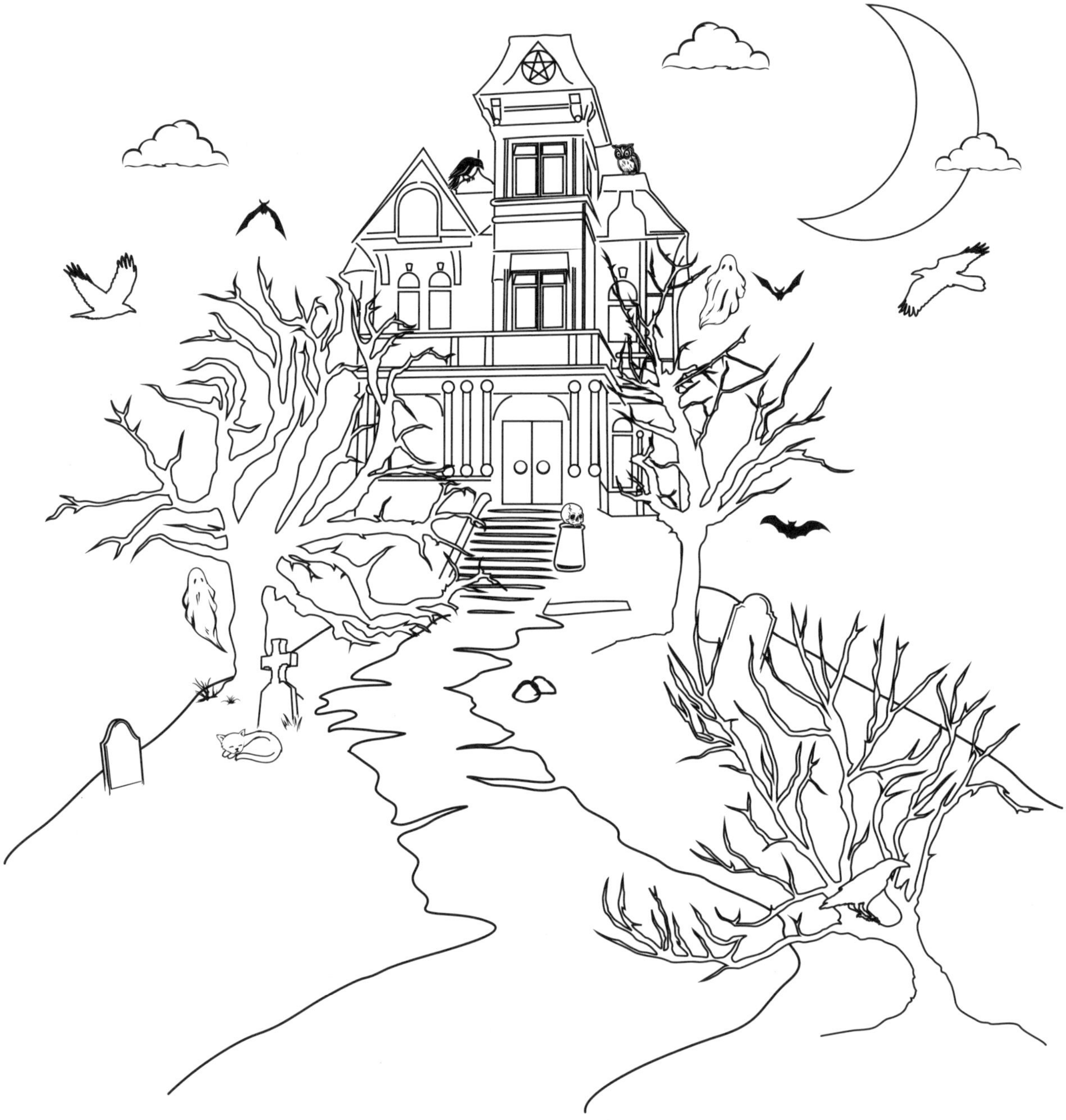

SPOT THE DIFFERENCE
HAUNTED HOUSE
SHARP-EYED SHENANIGANS!

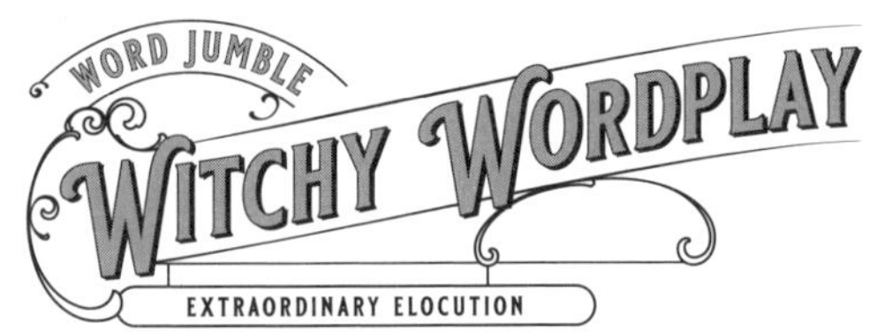

Feeling fantastical? Unscramble the witchy words below!

1. EVOCN
2. DHXEE
3. UNCDOLAR
4. OTBOCKRSIM
5. MIIRGOER
6. AOLKWCR
7. YSROERC
8. MIRFAALI
9. OUJECRN
10. GSIIL
11. SURCE
12. ALENCD
13. HMARC
14. KLABC GMAIC
15. YAMLECH

A pale horse approaches bearing an ominous rider! No time to dilly-dally; beat a hasty retreat and flee the maze before Death catches up with you!

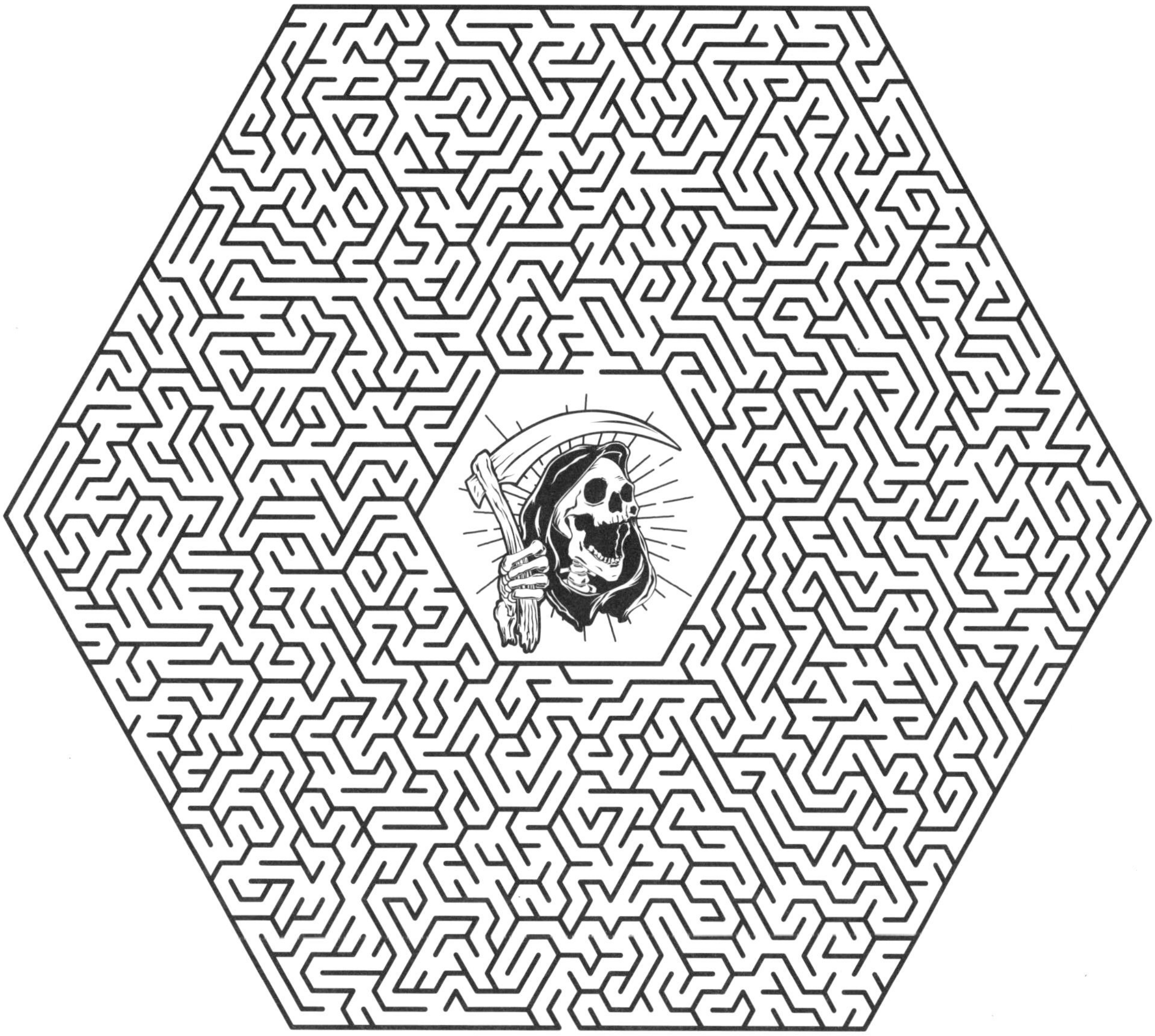

Homographs are words with the same spelling, but different meanings (and sometimes different pronunciations) depending on context.

For example, an incorporeal spirit AND suddenly going no-contact with a former acquaintance would both be appropriate uses of the word "ghost."

Write in the correct answer that matches both clues below.

1. A piece of sporting equipment *or* Dracula's alternate flying form:

____

2. Internet nickname *or* a spider's output:

____

3. A group of ravens *or* a secret plot:

____

4. An opening *or* causing a state of altered consciousness:

____

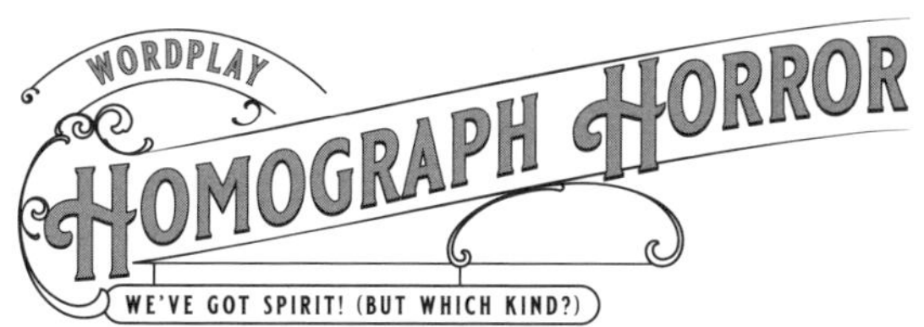

5. A witch's companion *or* someone you're acquainted with:

____

6. A place for a corpse *or* something very serious:

____

7. A psychic *or* a Starbuck's Grande:

____

8. Popular with witches *or* English teachers:

____

Revenge is a dish best served piping hot from a bubbling cauldron! Compose a haiku about a hex you have bestowed — or *wish* you had bestowed — upon a nemesis on the lines below.

Tip: Haiku is a Japanese poetic form comprised of three lines. The first line has five syllables, the second line has seven syllables, and the last line has five syllables.

____

____

____

LIKE YETI'S INSTA?

CRYPTOGRAM

NO. CRYPTOGRAM, NOT CRYPTIDGRAM.

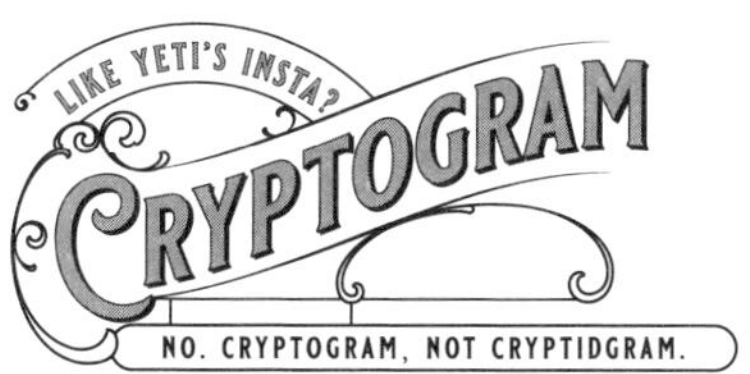

Decode the message! Each letter in the phrase has been replaced with a random number. Try to decode the message using the clues that have already been revealed!

A	B	C	D	E	F	G	H	I	J	K	L	M	N	O	P	Q	R	S	T	U	V	W	X	Y	Z
														18					17						

	O							
26	18	19	21	25	6	2	4	20

16	26	6	20	25	12	9	2	26	3		25

					O				T
21	25	6	20	10	18	6	20	26	17

	O									T
11	18	6	17	20	19	3	20	2	12	17

O									O			O		'	T
18	26		21	20	26		15	9	18		15	18	26	'	17

T					“		O	”			O				
17	25	7	20			26	18			5	18	19		25	26

25	26	12	15	20	19

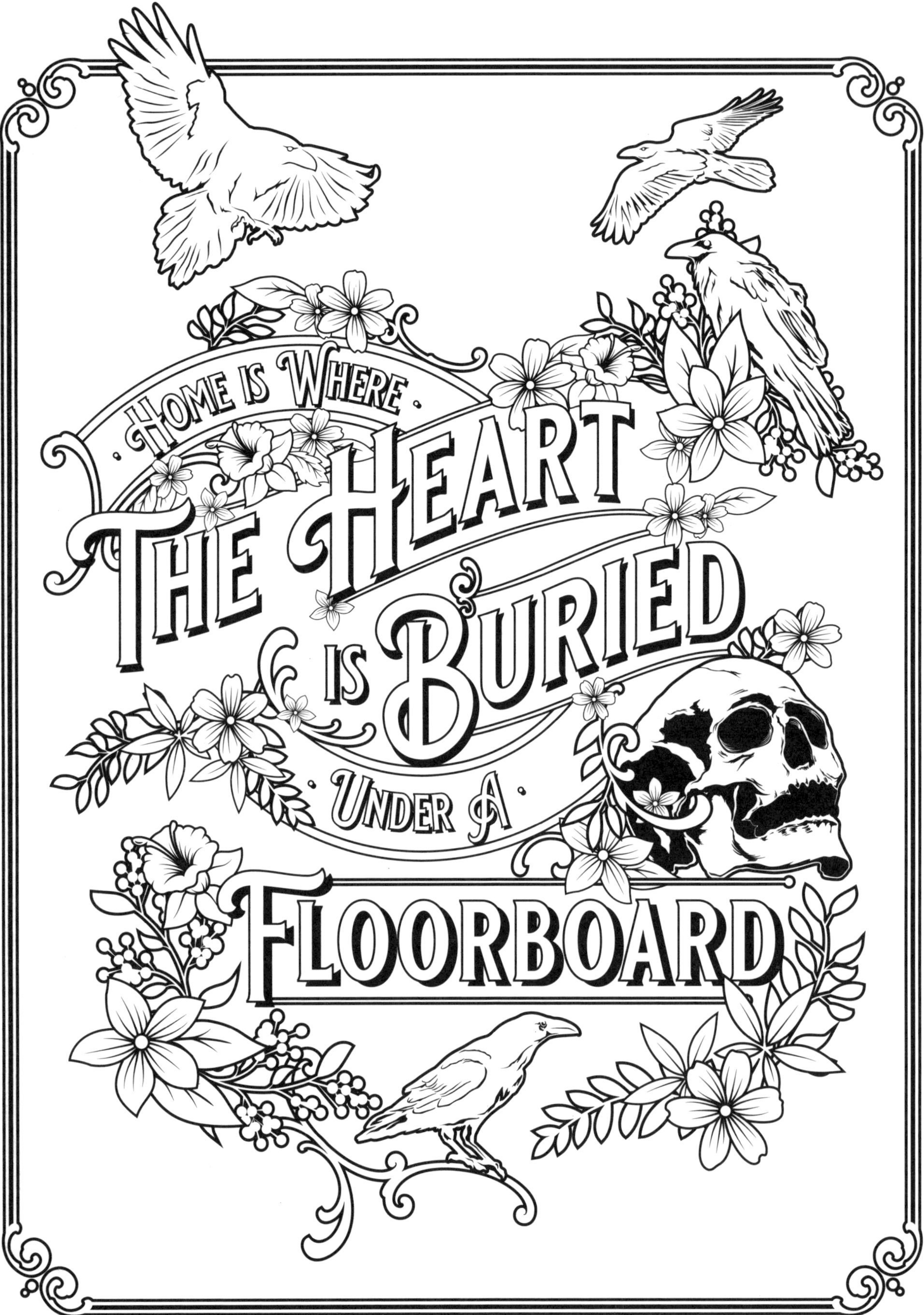
Home is Where
The Heart
is Buried
Under A
Floorboard

This game is a perfect companion to your next horror movie night. See which horror movies help you get to bingo fastest!

Jump scare	Monster appears to be vanquished but rises up again	Characters run upstairs to escape instead of out the front or back door	The "slutty" one gets killed first	Creepy kid
Self-defense weapon is juuuust out of reach	Someone goes to investigate an ominous sound	Foolish teens go into a cemetery or haunted house	No one has a cell phone or cell service	Can't find the car keys or the car won't start
Something evil is seen in or escapes from a mirror	Eyes change to indicate altered state or otherwise non-human characteristics	FREE SPACE	Characters clumsily fleeing in terror, tripping and falling	Masked slasher
Everyone decides to split up instead of sticking together	Blood is magical or possesses otherwise supernatural properties	Science gone wrong (e.g. mad scientist, genetically altered super spiders, etc.)	Final girl survives	Occultist explains what's going on to other characters
Angry spirits are involved	Someone gets possessed by a nefarious entity	Plot features a seemingly invincible monster	Key plot points take place in an abandoned building of some kind	Cursed object does cursed object things

Think you've got the fright stuff? Pair the movie quote with the classic horror film it's from by drawing a line connecting the two below!

1. "Listen to them, the children of the night. What music they make!"
2. "Tell her to stay away from the light."
3. "Be afraid. Be very afraid."
4. "It's alive! It's alive!"
5. "Do you like scary movies?"
6. "We all go a little mad sometimes."
7. "They're coming to get you, Barbara."
8. "There'll be food and drink and ghosts... and perhaps even a few murders. You're all invited."
9. "Your wife has such a beautiful neck..."
10. "To a new world of gods and monsters!"

The Fly

Scream

The House on Haunted Hill

Night of the Living Dead

Poltergeist

Bride of Frankenstein

Nosferatu

Frankenstein

Dracula

Psycho

Hollywood is calling and they want to bring your terrifying movie idea to life! Pitch your idea for a spooky film below:

TITLE (What are we calling this thing?)

TAGLINE (Give marketing a slogan to sell it.)

SUB-GENRE (Is it a horror-comedy? Slasher? True crime? Creature feature? How will this frightening cinematic masterpiece be categorized when it hits streaming platforms?)

PLOT SUMMARY (What's it about? Give 'em the ol' elevator pitch!)

CAST (Who will bring your characters to life on screen? A-list stars? Your childhood besties?)

SOUNDTRACK (Every great movie has a great soundtrack! Which songs will be in yours?)

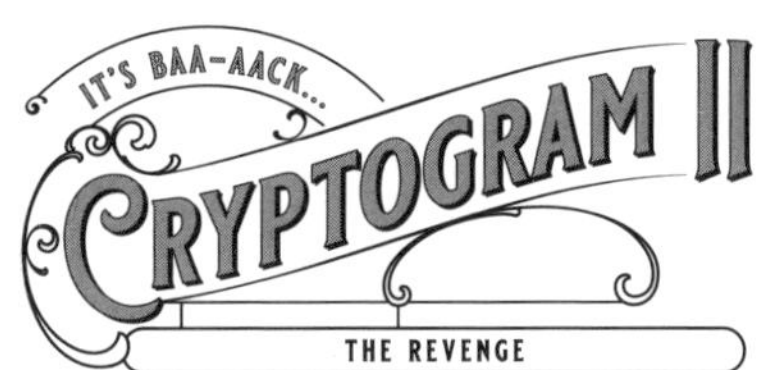

Decode the message! Each letter in the phrase has been replaced with a random number. Try to decode the message using the clues that have already been revealed!

A	B	C	D	E	F	G	H	I	J	K	L	M	N	O	P	Q	R	S	T	U	V	W	X	Y	Z
								18											15						

				'								I			
22	23	,	18		11		22	23	15		10	18	22	16	,

(Row 1 letters: — — , I' — — — T — I — — ,)

I	'								T			I		
18		11		12		8	16	22	15	13	7	18	16	2

					I	T						T				
23	26	4		3	18	15	8	19		8	13	15		23	10	10

									I			T			
10	7	23	11		11	20		7	18	21	19	15	10	13	26

24	23	3	16	7	2		12	22	4

T								I			
15	7	12	24	24	16	4		18	22		12

				I								
10	7	12	21	18	26	16		19	13	11	12	22

10	23	7	11

The answers to each riddle below are two words that rhyme. The first letters from each answer are revealed to help you solve the puzzle.

Example: a friend who's been cut up into pieces would be a "bloody buddy."

1. A plump winged critter:

F______________ B______________

2. A trolley or light rail, but with Satanic flair:

P______________ T______________

3. Sorcery when the magic isn't working quite right:

W______________ G______________

4. A pile of villains:

C______________ H______________

5. It makes a mode of corpse transport unlucky:

H______________ C______________

6. A phantasm who invites you to dinner:

G______________ H______________

7. A lazy animal who loves to wear black:

G______________ S______________

8. A stylish, popular monster:

C______________ G______________

9. An erotic curse:

S______________ H______________

10. A demonic Southern babe:

H______________ B______________

You'll need to call upon your knowledge of ancient mythology to tackle this puzzle!

ACROSS:

4. Malicious possessing spirits from Hebrew mythology

8. Location associated with Norse gods

9. Egyptian god of the dead and the underworld

10. Faust made a deal with him

12. Night goddess sometimes depicted as dressed in a black cloak made of stars

13. Demons are rumored to smell like it

16. Sumerian succubus, sometimes referred to as the first wife of Adam

17. Wish-granter, often trapped in a lamp

18. Greek triple goddess associated with magic, necromancy, and passage ways

20. Deity allegedly worshipped by the Knights Templar

24. The favored fruit of Persephone, Queen of the Greek underworld

26. A group of demons

27. Greek goddess of revenge

DOWN:

1. Shape-shifting Scottish water demon

2. Medusa, for example

3. The sin that got Lucifer cast out of Heaven

4. Thanatos' domain

5. Egyptian goddess depicted as a fierce lioness

6. Christmas demon of Germanic origin

7. Author best known for creating the Cthulhu Mythos

11. River that leads to Hades' domain

14. Sea serpent referenced in Biblical texts

15. Dionysus' domain

19. Three-headed dog who guards the entrance to the underworld

21. Sometimes referred to as the "Lord of the Flies"

22. Norse god associated with mischief

23. What Annabelle appears to be

25. Animal whose features are often associated with the Greek god Pan

You're the true crime detective! Pair the infamous serial killers listed with the number of victims they dispatched from this mortal coil using the handy chart on the opposite page. You'll find their dossiers below.

The Rogues Gallery

"Masked" Marco Martinez
- Active in Miami, Florida in the 1990s
- Left hockey a puck at the crime scene as a calling card
- Wore a hockey mask in honor of his favorite fictional killer

"Dreaded" Donovan Grant
- Active in Manchester, England in the 1990s
- All of his victims were men
- Arrested in 2000 but died before being convicted

Sal "The Slasher" Marini
- Active in Sicily, Italy in the 1920s
- Motivated by revenge; killed whoever crossed him
- Wore a Venetian carnival mask to hide his identity

"Bloodsucking" Bart Hart
- Active in 19th century London, England
- Drained victims of their blood
- Left roses at the crime scene as a calling card

Tabitha "Stabby Tabby" Thorn
- Active in Miami, Florida in the early 1980s
- Killed only ex-boyfriends who cheated on her
- Arrested & convicted in 1988

"Cannibal" Esther Goldman
- Active in 1960s Germany
- Killed & ate ex-Nazis to avenge family lost in WWII
- Arrested in the 1970s but never convicted

"Violent" Violet Hall
- Active in Portland, Oregon in the 1970s
- Left violets at the crime scene as a calling card
- Arrested & convicted in 1985

Alright, super sleuth — you've read their bios, now pair this murderer's row with their respective bodycounts using the clues below!

THE CLUES

- The least prolific killer was a woman
- The fourth least prolific killer was arrested but not convicted
- All killers who were active in England killed fewer than 20 people
- The most prolific killer was a woman
- The second most prolific killer wore a mask
- The third most prolific killer has a 2-syllable first name and killed in the United States
- The fourth most prolific killer had only male victims
- The two least prolific killers were motivated by vengeance
- All female American killers had an even number for their body count

	34	24	19	17	12	11	6
BLOODSUCKING BART							
SAL THE SLASHER							
MASKED MARCO							
STABBY TABBY							
CANNIBAL ESTHER							
VIOLENT VIOLET							
DREADED DONOVAN							

Barrett the Butcher has killed his annoying neighbors and hidden their corpses in the basement. Solve the puzzle below to determine how many bodies are down there!

+ + = 48

× = 0

÷ =

=

+ + + =

÷ = ?

If this cauldron's a-bubblin', don't come a-troublin'! Fill your cauldron with the ingredients in this word search to cast your latest spell.

```
J A X G G N M Z T S T S C Q K V R T C H V F O Q C A Z Q O J
L F L A C M U K M S G A B B L Y E A W A S H J D N Z W Q U Q
B T D Q P N C N V O I I Z D D F E R G Q N R A X P W N E D T
L R S B H O D A Q O M P D Y T H W R B S H V C U T X B M W N
O M T A I Q M G N D J S W O D D W T P E V W X Z P A W Z I Y
O W F U W W J Q B D T I Q V P U A B H U N M P Y B T H S V M
D F V N R O Q U J M L G G Z T K M L F S T A Y E B X I P C W
U J M F T I N J T O V E F L A M E Y B V F S L L E L S I R H
F Q W Z T N F R A N K I N C E N S E M Y Q Z K L C J K N T T
T W O O K Y K K E L C G Z M U E Z Y I S C A L E S Z E M F B
C W Q P S Z X S R C R U Y Y P O L Z U D G Z E K O A R E O O
K A U S T B X K I P B Y X H L U M B I M J R P K A P I A R N
S P A P T V P Z E G J Q M X F N U J O A S P W T J O U O N E
M G R T P B N M L E I B E W L L M G V N F K T G B S J Z U S
V J T A D U H Q D W F L H U H W L S E D A H T K O K M E K E
Y F Z X Y P Y E E R I J X J E J I C F R L M H M R R D J Q E
Z A X P V O B R R N Q V R F M Z W I R A U A S U O S R C L N
N A A Z I A S A F O X C U R L B G F S K Y O T G F H K L D S
E P X S A G E O L C M U C X O A T D I E J M G W B K X O Z R
K N E T T L E H O Z T M D B C M Z D P H G D K O Y N R V O I
N T M Q U T G F W C H W L E K W J U R D A R B R P N E E O C
E Y J U E Y N Z E R I Z O L N N H C K T Y I F T P G O H R D
T G P J Q Y Z H R L S G L L Y B B I O F Z K R B Y Z A D W C
Y S N P Q S Y V C A T O A A Y E K B P V M R E G H N O V A C
J S W M Y C Z P Y M L O V D G T N L T E N W V J S M V A O I
E X G Z D F K Z N V E F E O F K M V F C T M V O A K L W L E
X M I X Y H X X J I T S N N V F J O K M H A V W L T J J I G
V W G R P H N K J C W G D N D Z W L G X Z F L L T M J U F R
M M M C N M W O H L I O E A N Z A T Y F G S Z S X W Z D L V
D C K X R F N V R E B M R U U V C W H K Q G T I I W U O I K
```

sigil
belladonna
thistle
hemlock
elderflower
candle
frankincense
blood
mugwort
lavender
bones
scales
ash
whisker
nettle
hair
mandrake
petals
sage
clove
flame
salt
verbena
quartz

Fill in the blanks below with the missing word or phrase. Then plug those words into the corresponding blanks on the next page to complete the obituary. *(Note: You can do this one alone, but it's also fun to do with a necromancer!)*

1. Noun ______________________
2. Place ______________________
3. Place ______________________
4. Place ______________________
5. Verb ending in -ING ______________________
6. Plural noun ______________________
7. Noun ______________________
8. Adjective ______________________
9. Verb ______________________
10. Plural noun ______________________
11. Adjective ______________________
12. Noun ______________________
13. Noun ______________________
14. Female celebrity ______________________
15. Noun ______________________
16. Noun ______________________
17. Animal ______________________
18. Adjective ______________________
19. Noun ______________________
20. Noun ______________________
21. Adjective ______________________
22. Plural noun ______________________

CELEBRATED PHILANTHROPIST THURSTON WENTWORTH III DEAD AT 87

Thurston Wentworth III, a(n) ______________ magnate, died on Saturday in ______________. Mr. Wentworth was born in __________, but spent most of his life in ___________, where he was known for ____________ ____________ among the local residents. Over the course of his life, Mr. Wentworth donated millions of dollars to charitable organizations, including the National ____________________ Foundation.

Those who worked with Mr. Wentworth described him as a(n) ______________ man who never missed an opportunity to ____________ ______________.

Friends and family will always remember Mr. Wentworth for his ______________ ______________ and love of ________________(s).

Mr. Wentworth married ____________________________, a woman he met at university while studying _____________. They had two children, Thurston IV and Contessa, who still run the family ________________ business to this day. Mr. Wentworth is survived by his two children and his pet ______________.

Funeral services for Mr. Wentworth will be held at the ______________ ______________ Mortuary. Those wishing to honor Mr. Wentworth's memory are invited to make a donation to the ______________ Society, a ________________ charity that the Wentworth family has selected in recognition of Mr. Wentworth's love of _____________.

In each puzzle below and on the next page, two headlines are real and one is completely made up. See if you can identify the fake headline in each grouping!

PUZZLE 1

a.) 'Pistol-packing cheer mom' plotted the murder of her ex-husband's mother

b.) Kansas mother charged with killing teen daughter's boyfriend for not returning calls

c.) "Doomsday cult" mom is charged with first-degree murder in Idaho

PUZZLE 2

a.) California woman who faked her own kidnapping sentenced to 18 months in prison

b.) Adolescent kidnapped twice by the same man years apart

c.) Man sentenced to 1 year in prison for kidnapping prized show poodle

PUZZLE 3

a.) Dad started a sex cult at Sarah Lawrence College

b.) Memphis, Tennessee woman allegedly killed man because it was 'time to feed her demons'

c.) Satanic cult leader recruited teens working at Dairy Queen

PUZZLE 4

a.) Portland, Oregon stripper charged with murdering rival dancer in jealous rage

b.) OnlyFans model arrested in boyfriend's murder at Miami high-rise

c.) Man who began male stripper revue pleads guilty to homicide, racketeering charges

PUZZLE 5

a.) New York grandmother charged with masterminding jewel heist and double homicide

b.) Star sommelier arrested after authorities say video captures him setting fires at New York restaurants

c.) Shooters fled on scooters after shooting 10 people in alleged gang hit in New York

PUZZLE 6

a.) Oklahoma pastor's wife plotted his murder amid love triangle

b.) *How to Murder Your Husband* writer on trial for allegedly killing husband

c.) Texas woman confesses to killing husband because he 'complained about her cooking'

PUZZLE 7

a.) Security firm head had double life as leader of thieving, murdering gang

b.) Telecom CEO killed in plane crash was bankrolling drug empire, feds say

c.) Indiana insurance executive charged with operating sex trafficking ring

PUZZLE 8

a.) Husband sentenced to 65 years for killing wife in 'Fitbit murder'

b.) Miami, Florida woman charged with murder-for-hire plot orchestrated on Instagram

c.) Florida man tried to track his robbery victim by attaching an iPhone to his car

A
WOMAN'S
PLACE
is in a
COVEN
GOODBYE

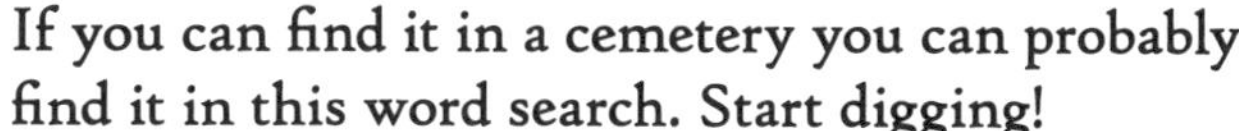

If you can find it in a cemetery you can probably find it in this word search. Start digging!

```
I M C P Y U W X X I B M I R S V N T Y V R Z K S E T V G G Q
D B A H J R N X G U C O F F I N O D G Z V V U I X H E R P L
B Y R U N N H P D D I K P H D J X F T K R Q B N R K P I X V
U V T B S S Y L B S X G V H C T E N C M D Q V D N S T M F F
U F W H N O B I N T C R F F H M P S G A B V U I N P F R M L
W Y U T B O L P I J O A C D D K I L L I S P W W D L K E U Z
U D Z W S W Z E F T R V K D P H T C P S W K F T T L B A Q N
P F S D N R E L U K P E A J E P A O H Q H W E B J X D P Q J
X R Z H E W K K P M S T R K M B P B Q E U Q A T W A E E V K
M B U L C O N C D Q E S W X W R H X P M A Q B C O R R R O X
B O E K R L N E Y Z O E J P I G H E N J Z R E K W D G E S C
G P R H O P R M P X I H L A R Z F D L C P U S P A T Z L Z M
N K Y W P D J E N K Q Y V W S Y Q I N G E R Q E V O L R E M
G T Q I O C Q T H U N U G N K C O H Y H I Y O A M M E M U U
H O X D L A J E B Q Z K T A A D W S D C E P W C E B O L L X
K K X O I M S R R M Y S E M L U O V N D G A B T E V G R O S
N H Y W S F Q Y P Z J U J D C C A J H H F C D S G S M R G G
T U P C I D I N L Y N B S K M G K S F E I S R S M O S F Y P
Y X W O T A P T W H P M O U R N E R A U O Q O G T I G I U L
Y R V I A H H B P K R N Q W Z S R W C R A D X G T O H V O N
Q X S I E M T Y W R O D O M R K I C M F C Z Z V V D N U T N
D N P K M X C X B M Q T J W D A U V L M Q O M Y N G P E O S
R E K C I F F Y Q O O D K Y W H K X M F V K P H J Z E E B G
H E E A J F C C N R Z F U N E R A L M N X R B H H B T P M G
C Z N A I U K D W T X F Z X O Y G G C L B O E U A V I G I L
O P H E Y D Q E Y U E T F D R S N E A R B O O B R G S V H D
R E W M O S M A S A B O F B X F U E G Z Y T L F U I U J K B
R K T Q F Y X D Q R Z P A R N R M F O L W P G M C S A S N Y
E I U O Q V G M C Y U F B Q L X Q B M U A N T C L Q B L U H
Q S S F R P V O B D L E C Z Y L Z R Q M G V J H J D L W R H
```

grave	funeral	coffin	eulogy
tomb	cemetery	headstone	widow
vigil	crypt	corpse	mortuary
casket	epitaph	sarcophagus	urn
mausoleum	burial	dead	grim reaper
hearse	necropolis	mourner	procession

Each riddle below is about a famous monster from movies or literature (or both). Guess which one each is about!

1. Out of my coffin, hungry all too often. I used to be brighter, but now I'm a bit of a biter.

Creature: ______________________

2. The woods in the dark can be quite scary; if I'm on the loose things could get hairy.

Creature: ______________________

3. I've been known to fly, but I'm also an intimidating guy.
If you look me in the eyes, I can mesmerize.

Creature: ______________________

4. When it comes to the social scene I'm kind of a fixture,
but whatever you do, don't look at my picture.

Creature: ______________________

5. Not quite dead, what happened to my head? I'd trade all my riches not to be in stitches.

Creature: ______________________

6. I'm kept under wraps, but I escaped from my tomb.
If you encounter me you'll meet your doom!

Creature: ______________________

7. My visage is a shock, some say my work rocks!
I'd still be a thing of dread if I hadn't lost my head.

Creature: ______________________

8. When the Doctor's not in, it's time to sin! I can get kind of wild, but my alter-ego is mild.

Creature: ______________________

Each string of letters below is the scrambled name of a different cryptozoological marvel. Unscramble them to identify these fictitious fauna and solve the puzzle!

1. HOLC SENS OTEMSNR ______
2. ANTMHMO ______
3. QSUAHCAST ______
4. PACURAHCBA ______
5. IMANLABOEB WANNSMO ______
6. EESRJY LVIED ______
7. MIDEMAR ______
8. OWGEIND ______
9. NARMUITO ______
10. NUPIYB ______
11. ACJLAEOKP ______
12. ASGEUPS ______
13. RENAKK ______
14. ROFWLEWE ______
15. TEHEIPAFSRSH ______

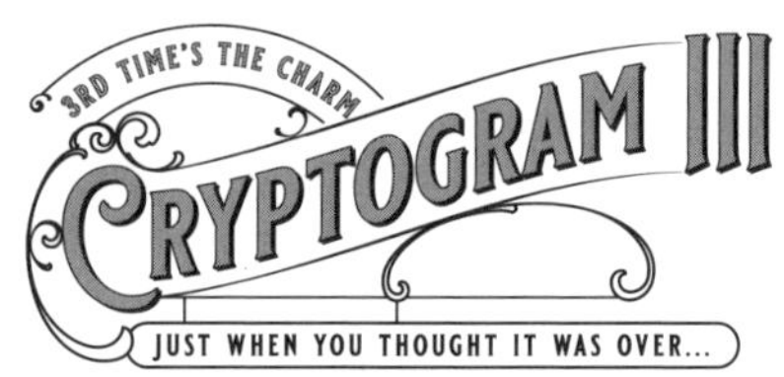

Decode the message! Each letter in the phrase has been replaced with a random number. Try to decode the message using the clues that have already been revealed!

A	B	C	D	E	F	G	H	I	J	K	L	M	N	O	P	Q	R	S	T	U	V	W	X	Y	Z
22																			9						

_ _ (1 24)   _ _ (5 18)   _ _ _ T (24 6 15 9)   _ _ _ _ (17 1 7 6)

_ ' _ (1 ' 5)   _ _ _ _ _ _ (26 11 5 1 24 19)   _ A _ _ (4 22 26 25)

A _ (22 12)   A _ (22 24)   _ _ _ _ _ _ _ (11 5 1 24 11 3 12)

_ A _ _ (10 22 16 25)   _ _ _ T (5 1 12 9)

Are you Hell-bent for horror? Titillated by terror? Does trepidation make you tingle? Compose a haiku about your favorite scary story on the lines below!

Tip: Haiku is a Japanese poetic form comprised of three lines. The first line has five syllables, the second line has seven syllables, and the last line has five syllables.

____

____

____

A rebus puzzle combines pictures and individual letters to depict a word or phrase. Solve the puzzles below and on the opposite page to reveal the spooky answers!

1. + =

2. + =

3. + + =

4. + + + =

PETRIFYING PUZZLES
REBUS RITUAL
PRETERNATURALLY PICTURESQUE

5.  + M + $ =

6.  +  =

7. C +  =

8.  + IN +  =

To spell the answer to each puzzle below and on the next page you'll have to find the letters in the clues provided! *(Hint: None of the answer words have a repeated letter within them.)*

PUZZLE 1

- The first letter is in MAGE but not in GRIMOIRE ________
- The second letter is in MACABRE but not in MENACE ________
- The third letter is in GHOST but not in GHOUL ________
- The fourth letter is in HELL but not in BLOODTHIRSTY ________
- The fifth letter is in but not in MONSTER but not MYSTERY ________
- The sixth letter is in OMINOUS but not in MAUSOLEUM ________
- The seventh letter is in ARCANE but not in FRANKENSTEIN ________

PUZZLE 2

- The first letter is in CREEP but not in PENTAGRAM ________
- The second letter is in CASKET but not in PYROKINETICS ________
- The third letter is in RITUAL but not in ASTRAL ________
- The fourth letter is in ASTRAL but not in SHAPESHIFTER ________
- The fifth letter is in DEATH but not in TELEPATHY ________
- The sixth letter is in SPIDER but not in LUPINES ________
- The seventh letter is in GOTHIC but not in CHILLING ________
- The eighth letter is in CEREMONY but not in CEMETERY ________

PUZZLE 3

- The first letter is in FUNERAL but not in VENGEFUL ________
- The second letter is in SIGIL but not in GORGONS ________
- The third letter is in DRACULA but not in MARAUDER ________
- The fourth letter is in HELL but not in SPELL ________
- The fifth letter is in SÉANCE but not in SANCTUM ________
- The sixth letter is in AMULET but not in SUPERNATURAL ________
- The seventh letter is in SORCERY but not in CORPSE ________

PUZZLE 4

- The first letter is in CONJURE but not in OUIJA ________
- The second letter is in BIZARRE but not in ZOMBIE ________
- The third letter is in SPOOKY but not in SPELLBOOK ________
- The fourth letter is in CREEPY but not in NECROMANCY ________
- The fifth letter is in IMMORTAL but not in FAMILIAR ________
- The sixth letter is in LAIR but not in PARANORMAL ________
- The seventh letter is in MURDER but not in MYSTERIOUS ________

PUZZLE 5

- The first letter is in ENCHANT but not in INCANTATION ________
- The second letter is in APPARITION but not in POTION ________
- The third letter is in GHOUL but not in GHOSTLY ________
- The fourth letter is in POISON but not in SPIRIT ________
- The fifth letter is in HEADSTONE but not in SHADOW ________
- The sixth letter is in CURSE but not in CRYPTS ________
- The seventh letter is in DEATH but not in HEART ________

PUZZLE 6

- The first letter is in COBWEBS but not in SUCCUMB ________
- The second letter is in HEX but not in BAPHOMET ________
- The third letter is in DOOMED but not in MEDIUM ________
- The fourth letter is in NEFARIOUS but not in FIENDS ________
- The fifth letter is in MALICIOUS but not in MEDUSA ________
- The sixth letter is in HYPNOSIS but not in LYCANTHROPY ________
- The seventh letter is in SATAN but not in PHANTOM ________
- The eighth letter is in TALISMAN but not in PENTACLE ________

You don't need second sight to see these spooksters! Just a keen eye, sharp wits, and the will to pierce the veil between this mortal coil and the realm that lies beyond are needed to spot the specters in this word search.

```
Y A I R T S P O O K Y Y F A U W Y Z B M E C U W Q F G O Q Y
P I P W F L U S K E L E T O N C T N Y Z D V T C T E K C O O
M R G Y Q E U G B M W Z B S P M X P B Z M F X Q E C G G X L
A J W U S S O D X D X Z J I R O P F R D U Z F Y T T W M L I
H O R M D O U J P T E G Y M R B L E D E T R U Q B O O K M X
X I A C C H I L L I N G V N Q N I T W A S E H N K P C I V H
N Q I A M M E P U Y M X K Z E H C H E H H E J L N L Y L K D
X A T S J F X S Q V D H R C X B D G S R Z N N D A A K M Q K
K T H O P W J B G R A V E Y A R D B C A G G L C N S E M G A
J G Y S E E Z R F S Z E I X P I E A X S G E S L E M A B C Z
T U S H F X C B L F V R L G B W Z Z D T K N I M X R G K R D
X N P P A C K T M F H W L G E C T N W R Y X H S Z G W Q E Q
V J I V Z U U P E H C O E H H Z T Q P A L V C P T D T Y E O
D X R S R T N M C R U A F K A R Y M U L S H A D O W Y J P M
A G I P E K M T U T S W M S I M P E K P X F B Z T M O B Y I
P H T O N E T W E I D L H F W B N I R L X B P H A N T O M N
P U U E B U K C P D P D E M A V T K Z A X E S N K N K G I X
A V Q C D S A D A O T L Q T E P U U F N Q M W K O K S X V Y
R F T I T N E V D I B W A D A B R W N E Q L R Y R C F O D Y
I C O Z S O Z H T I U R M N O F N M P K P W Y B S J S U P A
T Y G A R K A E M P S H B M C N E C R O M A N C Y A P S P X
I P E U S C I B S H Y T N T K H O H X I K U T X N L B J S O
O E P F E H H U A A O S U O S C E W B T P N B S O U J U V H
N R Q G A E Y T B N X T P R N U T T A G U O Q Y U O Q Q L B
F Z V H N X Q N C T D P C G B Y K O T V L O I G I K F W R Q
W I F O C J H B M A G O J E T A Z D E E O P D P J Z X G P K
Y U Y S E B D E X S W U N L M J N D Q V K A Y N A A X R P E
Y H Z T O J P X R M F L H E A K B C D O F M W J D H L K C J
J B R Z X W C X P E A R G U D L V M E U M V L W J Q K A V O
J X F P U A K U P C N N H K J I C V H F B T Y I T N J F R P
```

ouija
graveyard
abandoned
phantom
astral plane
chilling
wraith
poltergeist
creepy
shadowy
presence
ectoplasm
disturbance
ghost
skeleton
haunted
spirit
necromancy
phantasm
séance
spooky
apparition
specter
planchette

Flex your creative muscles with the easiest of storytelling! Use the prompts below to distill these sinister story ideas into just two sentences.

Write a two-sentence short story about a ghost haunting a shopping mall:

Write a two-sentence short story about an incompetent demon:

Write a two-sentence short story about a child with telekinesis:

You've successfully subdued the demons who dwell on the land of an abandoned cabin... *for now.* Leave a note to passersby warning them not to rouse the diabolical evil that lurks here!

Fill in the blanks below with the missing word or phrase. Then plug them into the corresponding blanks on the next page to complete the message. *(Note: You can do this one alone, but it's also fun to do with the ancient deity of your choice.)*

1. Adjective ____________________
2. Adverb ____________________
3. Verb ____________________
4. Adjective ____________________
5. Liquid ____________________
6. Adjective ____________________
7. Noun ____________________
8. Adjective ____________________
9. Noun ____________________
10. Verb ____________________
11. Plural noun ____________________
12. Place ____________________
13. Plural noun ____________________
14. Noun ____________________
15. Adjective ____________________
16. Verb ____________________
17. Noun ____________________
18. Noun ____________________

TAKE HEED AND READ THESE WORDS OF WARNING!

If you've stumbled upon this message, you are in ______________ danger! This cabin sits atop a gateway to hell that can be opened all too ______________. The best thing you can do is leave at once and never ______________ again; your mere presence on this site may have already roused the ______________ creatures who dwell here and yearn to break free!

On the walls of this cabin, you will see a summoning spell scrawled in ______________. Whatever you do, do not utter these ______________ words! All it takes is one foolish visitor reciting those words to awaken the ______________.

I tried to burn this ______________ cabin to the ground, but alas, a powerful supernatural ______________ protects the cabin, making it impossible to destroy. I tried to alert the authorities, but they refused to ______________. I barely escaped with my own life, and then wrote this message to warn ______________.

Once the creatures rise from the bowels of ______________ little can be done to stop them. They will not rest until they have claimed the ______________ of every person they can find on these grounds. They will use all manner of trickery and ______________ to get what they want. Escape from their ______________ grip is nearly impossible once they have risen.

If you want to survive, ______________ for your life immediately and do not look back! The demons are counting on your ______________ to free them from their ______________!

You've been hired to host a weekly horror movie double-feature for a major TV network!

Craft your pitch for the network execs below (continued on the next page):

PICK A STAGE NAME

DESCRIBE YOUR HOST PERSONA *(What do you wear? Are you a sexy goth vixen? An arch, dapper, over-the-top scenery-chewer? A spooky ghoul with a penchant for puns?)*

THEME MUSIC *(Which song — or songs — appear in the show intro/outro?)*

CATCHPHRASE *(TV hosts often have a memorable catchphrase; what's yours?)*

DESCRIBE YOUR SET *(Haunted attic, forest campsite, mad scientist's lab? Where do you broadcast from?)*

SPECIAL GUESTS (*Are you inviting a co-host or special guests to interview between segments? Whether it's actors, filmmakers, or your favorite horror YouTubers, fill in the details below.)*

SCARY CINEMA (*Which frightful films are you excited to present to your new audience?)*

The answers to each riddle below are two words that rhyme. The first letters from each word are revealed to help you solve the puzzle.

Example: A freakout about The Devil would be a "satanic panic."

1. Dance party of the dead:

G______________ R______________

2. A slasher who has taken up meditation:

C______________ K______________

3. An ominous religious leader:

S______________ M______________

4. Dinner time for cryptids:

B______________ F______________

5. Ghosts having a fun day out are engaged in a:

H______________ J______________

6. A werewolf's complaint:

L______________ W______________

7. If Dracula wants to travel by air he'll need probably need to book a:

N______________ F______________

8. Zombie government agent:

U______________ F______________

9. Decor for your crypt:

L______________ F______________

10. Harry Potter has one of these on his forehead:

B______________ S______________

Each puzzle below and on the next page has a bit of bizarre advice with a spooky word hidden within. Find the hidden word in each one!

Example: *HavinG RAVEns for pets is only asking for trouble; I suggest a less mercurial familiar.*

1. “Want to maintain an appearance that’s youthful and exotic? Ask eternally beautiful creatures like vampires to reveal their secrets!”

____

2. “Need a break from your adult responsibilities? Try getting possessed and being host to an infernal entity for a change!”

____

3. “With the right amount of wit, charm, and scheming, anything you want can be yours!”

____

4. “No matter what occurs, educating yourself in the Dark Arts will always be a transferable skill.”

____

5. "You may want to stab at your enemies, but a hex is so much less traceable."

____

6. "When casting a hex on your adversary, what's vital is managing your expectations; their downfall may not be *immediate*, but it *will* be satisfying."

____

7. "If you find yourself near a siren cove, never allow yourself to listen to their song; next thing you know, you'll be drowning."

____

8. "Today is the day — take up necromancy, summon a dragon and go for a ride! Adventure awaits!"

____

Think you know it all when it comes to vampires? Put your knowledge of hematological hunger to the test with this bloody puzzle!

ACROSS:

2. General Mills cereal vampire

4. Blood-sucking fairy of the Scottish Highlands

7. Seaside home of the Lost Boys

8. Dracula's insect-eating henchman

12. Real-life person who may have been the inspiration for Dracula

14. Wooden object feared by vampires

15. Allium believed to repel vampires

16. Book series and film franchise known for its sparkly vampires

17. The first human to become a vampire, according to Greek mythology

19. 1985 Jim Carrey vampire comedy film

21. Mountain range that is home to Dracula's castle

23. Vampire movie starring David Bowie

24. Dracula's nemesis

25. Teenage vampire slayer

27. Star of Univeral's famed 1931 *Dracula* film

28. Hungarian noblewoman who allegedly drank the blood of virgins to preserve her youth

29. *Interview with the Vampire* author

DOWN:

1. Stephen King's 1975 vampire novel

3. Concrete Blonde album featuring "The Vampire Song"

5. The first vampire movie ever made

6. *Dark Shadows* protagonist

9. Irish author Joseph Thomas Sheridan Le Fanu's titular vampire character

10. Vampiric goat-killing cryptid

11. Vampires don't have one

13. Creature born of a union between a human and a vampire, according to Balkan folklore

18. A vampire's maker

20. John William Polidori's 1819 short story that inspired the vampires of modern fiction

22. Medical condition that gave rise to some vampire mythology

23. HBO's southern Gothic fantasy horror series that heavily featured vampires

26. Where vampires have been known to sleep

1
2
3
4
5
6
7
8
9
10
11
12
13
14
15
16
17
18
19
20
21
22
23
24
25
26
27
28
29

MAZE

Haunted Hollow

EVADE THE ENCHANTRESS!

Find your way out of the haunted forest and back to town before the witch finds you!

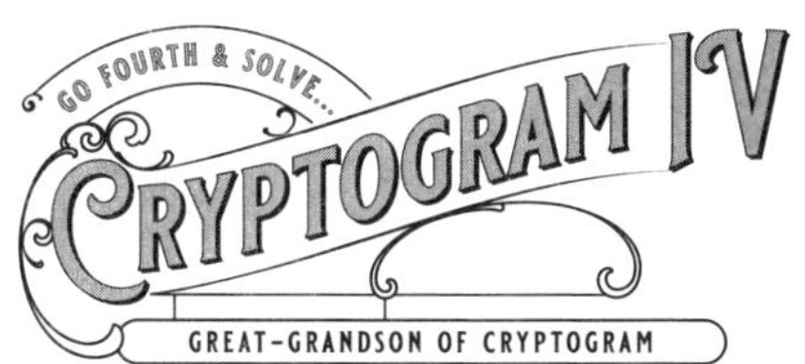

Decode the message! Each letter in the phrase has been replaced with a random number. Try to decode the message using the clues that have already been revealed!

A	B	C	D	E	F	G	H	I	J	K	L	M	N	O	P	Q	R	S	T	U	V	W	X	Y	Z
				14																				26	

_	E		_	_	E
11	14		21	9	14

_	_	_	_	_	_	Y	_	_	_
9	18	6	6	16	13	26	16	7	12

_	E	_	_	_	_	_	_	_	_	_
6	14	21	6	16	11	20	21	16	18	7

_	_	_	E	_	_	E	_		_	E	_	_	_
18	11	22	14	22	22	14	24		24	14	17	18	7

Y	_	_		_	E	E	_	E	_		_	_	E	_
26	18	20		7	14	14	24	14	24		25	9	14	7

Y	_	_		_	E	_	E		Y	_	_	_	_	E	_
26	18	20		25	14	6	14		26	18	20	7	12	14	6

Satan has hired you as his attorney and wants you to work on drafting an infernal contract for him. Fill in the blanks below with the missing word or phrase. Then plug those words into the corresponding blanks on the next page to complete the story. (*Note: You can do this one alone, but it's also fun to do with your coven.*)

1. Noun ______________________
2. Celebrity ______________________
3. Adjective ______________________
4. Adjective ______________________
5. Adjective ______________________
6. Adjective ______________________
7. Noun ______________________
8. Liquid ______________________
9. Period of time ______________________
10. Noun ______________________
11. Noun ______________________
12. Adjective ______________________
13. Adjective ______________________
14. Adjective ______________________
15. Adverb ______________________
16. Noun ______________________
17. Place ______________________
18. Adjective ______________________
19. Noun ______________________

THE CONTRACT

This Agreement is being entered into by Lucifer, Prince of ______________, hereto referred to as "Satan," and ______________, hereto referred to as "The Damned."

In exchange for The Damned's ____________________ Soul, Satan agrees to provide the following to The Damned:

1. ______________ good looks

2. ______________ wealth

3. A(n) ______________ career in ______________

The Agreement will commence once signed in _________________________ and remain in full force and effect of infernal law for eternity.

Satan will collect The Damned's Soul after a period of ________________, at which time the Soul will be brought to Hell for ______________________ and ______________________.

The Damned concurs this Agreement is exclusive and that their Soul will not be promised to another _______________________ entity.

Any modification to this _______________________ Agreement will require the prior written approval of Satan.

The Damned is of _________________________ mind and entering into this agreement ________________. The Damned has elected to waive their right to ______________ in order to expedite the execution of The Agreement.

This Agreement will be governed by the laws of ____________________ and disputes shall be settled by ___________________ ___________________.

REBUS REDUX

REAPER'S REBUS

REPREHENSIBLE REPRESENTATIONS

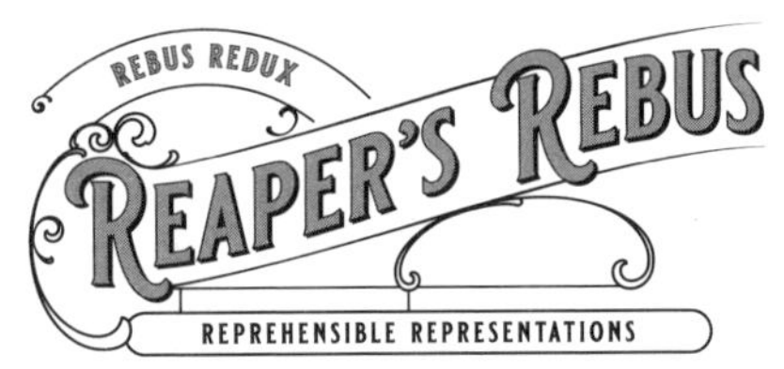

The puzzles below and on the opposite page pair pictures and letters to represent words. Solve them to reveal the ghastly answers!

1. 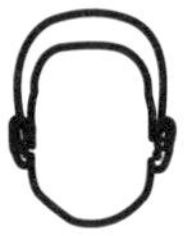 + 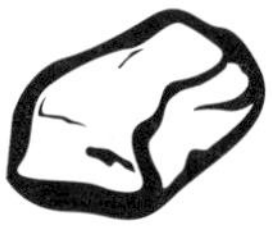 =

2. 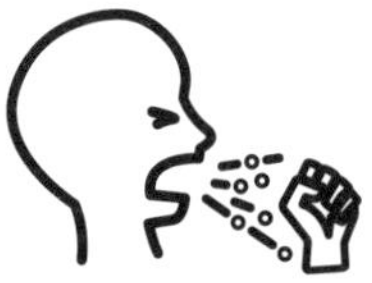 + 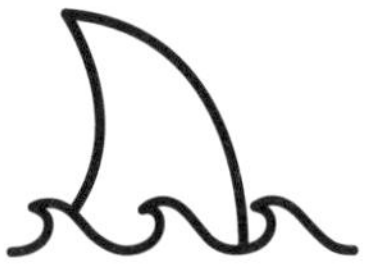 =

3. 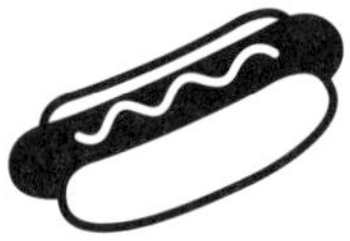 + IN + 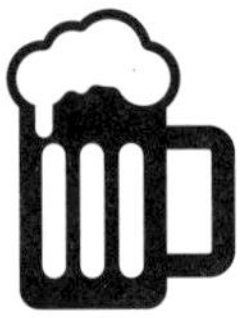 =

4. 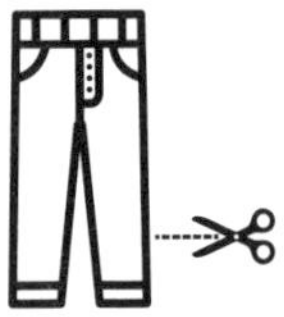 + 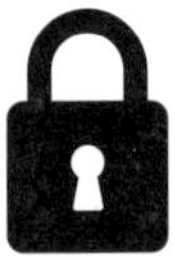 =

5. + + =

6. + TAXI =

7. + A A =

8. + P R + N D =

To conjure the answers to this bewitching cauldron of conundrums you'll need to know a thing or two about witches, both fictional and historic.

ACROSS:

2. Spell book

5. Warlock affiliated with the Romanov family

6. Tennessee witch who terrorized a 19th century farmer

9. Film that famously features the line "We are the weirdos, mister."

12. Sleeping Beauty's supernatural tormentor

17. Sorceress of Arthurian legend

18. The Good Witch in Oz

20. *The* _______ *Witch* by Anton LaVey

23. Rhode Island town featured in John Updike's witchy novel

24. Animal companion/servant

25. *The* _______ *Witch Project*

26. *Hocus Pocus* sisters

28. Enchanted liquid

DOWN:

1. Sea witch of *The Little Mermaid* fame

3. Literary work featuring the line "Double, double toil and trouble; Fire burn and cauldron bubble."

4. Disney witch who first appeared in the Donald Duck cartoon "Trick or Treat"

7. A witch's curse

8. Famed New Orleans Voodoo priestess

10. Massachusetts town notorious for being the site of witch trials in 1692

11. First woman accused during the 1692 witch trials

13. Sunnydale witch

14. Witchy mode of transport

15. *Bell, Book and Candle* witch

16. *The Addams Family* witch

19. Chicken-legged hut resident

21. Kettle typically used for spell casting, potion brewing, etc.

22. Samantha's mortal husband

27. Teenage witch

1
2
3
4
5
6
7
8
9
10
11
12
13
14
15
16
17
18
19
20
21
22
23
24
25
26
27
28

Hecate, the Goddess of Necromancy, is off to wake the dead. Solve the math puzzle below to see how many souls she raises from the grave!

× = 121

12 × = 132

20 − =

− = 7

× =

÷ = ?

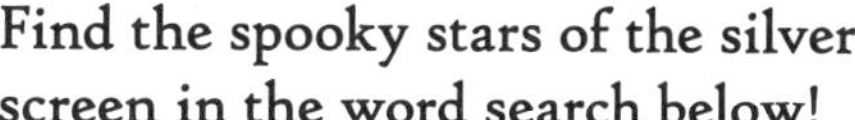
Find the spooky stars of the silver screen in the word search below!

Q J L P A C F B H Y G M J B H Z F C R I N L H P E M I D B K
L Z M I T A G S T P C N Y X W N O T O P O R W B B S A I V V
T Q S F O L Q Y R J A W S N M V O J J S S F V M S E S P M C
Z F N H D R I Q J H V G G P W U P Z R Y T I C P G H O U L G
M G F I N X H A E Y Z I R H E K V O O M S U Q E J B G V S O
L E Z Y J L H F A Y U E E W R V L K G M N K T T O W B L Q U
T Q Z X T Q M F L Y C X M Z H W P V I H B E D H A V X J B P
Y L N I R T W H G S R M L B I I H J R N K I L G S P R I K H
S O S O G M B A Y I X N I B G D B X G W V S E L O A L P I F
C U O D E M O N S R N M N E W L C R H R B I D I W F F U N A
F H M W E L P T C O Z B S V B J X Q U Z Q K S V W K F K G R
G A H D X Q T H B R L J B T G O F Q E V B R L I T I N E K S
G X Z H Y I W C E J E E P M I U R W Y T L I C N B Z B V O C
J I L B J N M G A K G A C D Q W R H K J O W C G F L Q N N E
C R J V N R M H S A G N T G U O R D G M B S Y D B Y E P G O
K T M V D W G A T A P C F U Y J F P R O D M N E M A X M C W
N D H T M I S L A S H E R E R P R R G A D C X A H E T R A B
O N U U R T S D B F F V V F M E N C A I C Z D D B J D H I N
W D S P L C F T Y X C K V G F N M Z P N C U I S B I C Y C O
D V G Z U H P D Y W P S H O Z N A I N Q K Z L L S W O D M I
M J E J G I U T G O Z R Z T F E E O Q J M E N A L J F E Z X
U J E T D U X X Z L J I Y G K O J J E W D P N W S A T V L F
L X O C E R A T W F V B O D Y S N A T C H E R S F B K D D A
H V X R F J J P P M L L R L M U M M Y P W V I R T N V K G A
N O S F E R A T U A S G B C W K I K V M O L P V U E Z G L R
T J A M J J F C E N Q J W Q R W L M G T X A T X W W I J R M
H C K I L L E R T Y M U A M S C G A C T H A I W S E P N P S
J C W R Y M L B B H A L I E N V F X M P W K T N S X Z O N M
J V G K B T F V Y Y W R S J X B P N O P X H V N F J Q T V E
O N Z H L D O Z G E P Z Q T Y N C U O P F F W K M S O G F N

Dracula
slasher
zombie
killer
creature
witch

living dead
demons
Bodysnatchers
Nosferatu
Mr. Hyde
Frankenstein

beast
Cthulhu
ghoul
King Kong
Gremlins
alien

Wolf Man
Godzilla
Jaws
Invisible Man
Blob
Mummy

Each clue below has an answer that ends with the first letter of the next clue's answer.

1. Sabbatic goat: ____________________

2. Mummy's spot: ____________________

3. Harbinger of death: ____________________

4. Some magical lockets: ____________________

5. Seer's stock and trade: ____________________

6. City of dead: ____________________

7. Arcane seal: ____________________

8. Ruled by the moon: ____________________

9. Like a puzzle: ____________________

10. A murder: ____________________

11. She-demon: ____________________

12. Endora's craft: ____________________

I REFUSE TO
REST IN PEACE
I EXPECT TO
HAUNT IN
RETRIBUTION

In each puzzle below and on the next page, two headlines are real and one is completely made up. See if you can identify the fake headline in each grouping!

PUZZLE 1

a.) Owner hired ghost hunters to perform séance for "haunted" pet shop

b.) Serial entrepreneur opens antique shop specializing in haunted artifacts

c.) "Haunted" doll returns to Houston family after being thrown out multiple times

PUZZLE 2

a.) Teacher accused of burning, cutting teens to expel demons

b.) "Satanic" haunted house described as "portal to Hell" finally knocked down

c.) Man who fatally stabbed wife not guilty by reason of demonic possession

PUZZLE 3

a.) Pentagon used extra terrestrial technology to develop weapons

b.) Pentagon to reveal truth about UFO files in rare Senate hearing

c.) Pentagon's secret UFO program investigated poltergeists

PUZZLE 4

a.) Ghostly floating city appears in China's skies

b.) Ghost solves ghastly Philadelphia murder

c.) Ghost suspected in arson case

PUZZLE 5

a.) Woman sues dry cleaner, claiming staff put a "hex" on her

b.) "Vampire" skeleton found pinned to ground with sickle around neck

c.) London family cleared of "exorcism" killing

PUZZLE 6

a.) Indonesia locks quarantine violators in "haunted house" as punishment

b.) Seattle hospital menaced by ghosts of pandemic victims

c.) Reports of paranormal activity increased during Coronavirus pandemic

PUZZLE 7

a.) "Human mermaid" sets record, holding breath under water for 34 minutes

b.) Park ranger survives seven lightning strikes

c.) "Human spider" climbs tallest skyscrapers without rope or climbing equipment

PUZZLE 8

a.) Couple claims CCTV shows "ghost of deceased tenant" in their home

b.) Dash cam footage captures image of alleged ghost hitchhiker

c.) Woman catches alleged "child spirit" throwing books in creepy video

You're the paranormal investigator! Pair the seven spooky specters listed below with their respective haunts using the handy chart on the opposite page. You'll find their dossiers below.

The Ghostly Gallery

Agatha
- b. 1831 in Surrey, England
- d. 1850; tuberculosis

William
- b. 1920 in Chicago, Illinois
- d. 1960; shot by his wife in jealous rage

Marie
- b. 1850 in southern France
- d. 1890; killed by unfaithful husband

Anne
- b. 1930 in London, England
- d. 1965; suicide

Sylvia
- b. 1945 in New York City
- d. 1965; hanged herself

Irving
- b. 1908 in Bridgeport, Connecticut
- d. 1950; heart attack at work

Oscar
- b. 1901 in Dublin, Ireland
- d. 1929; murdered in street stabbing

Alright, hunter of haunters — you've read their bios, now pair these spectral spooksters with their respective homes using the clues below!

The Clues

- The lighthouse ghost killed herself
- The hotel, castle, and pub ghosts were murdered
- The forest and pub ghosts are male
- The lighthouse, library, and manor ghosts are female
- The hotel ghost was older than both the pub and lighthouse ghosts at time of death
- The library ghost was born in America
- The castle ghost was born in Europe

	NEW ENGLAND LIGHTHOUSE	ENGLISH MANOR	UNIVERSITY LIBRARY	BRITISH PUB	ABANDONED CASTLE	FOREST	SEASIDE HOTEL
AGATHA							
WILLIAM							
MARIE							
SYLVIA							
OSCAR							
ANNE							
IRVING							

Help Sasquatch find his way home to his cave before poachers trap him!

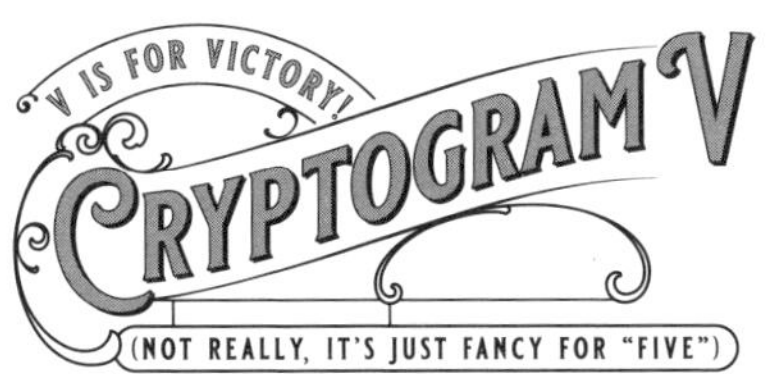

Decode the message! Each letter in the phrase has been replaced with a random number. Try to decode the message using the clues that have already been revealed!

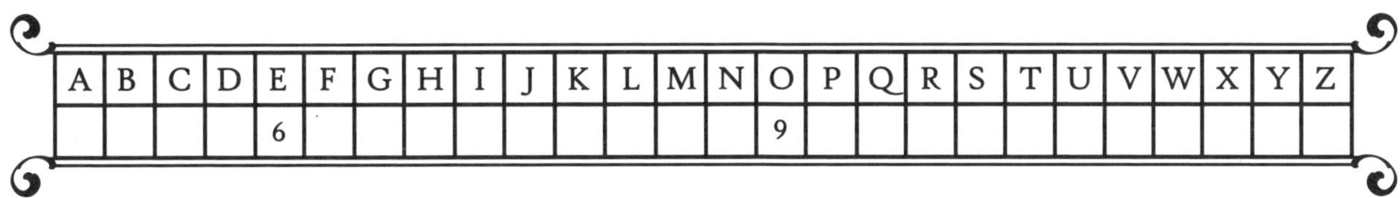

A	B	C	D	E	F	G	H	I	J	K	L	M	N	O	P	Q	R	S	T	U	V	W	X	Y	Z
				6										9											

	O	O												E
21	9	9	16		17	8	23	11	21	13		24	1	6

	O					;			E		’		E
19	9	14	23	11	21		17	8	6	4		1	6

				E				E			E				E
19	24	10	10	6	16		5	6	11	21	6	24	11	19	6

					E			O					
24	11	16		11	6	19	1	9	14	24	11	19	4

You're the magical matchmaker! Pair the familiars with their respective sorceress using the handy chart on the opposite page. You'll find details about the familiars below.

The Magical Menagerie

Cat
Small carnivorous mammal with pointy ears and furry coat. Ranges in size from 9-10" tall, and 8-14 pounds.

Pegasus
Mythological mammal appearing as a winged stallion. Pegasus is 67" tall, weighs 700 pounds, and is a vegetarian.

Wolf
Large omnivorous canine. Ranges in size from 29-36" tall, and weighs between 55-180 pounds.

Dragon
Mythological winged reptilian carnivore. Dragons can be at least 80" tall and weigh up to 3000 pounds.

Serpent
Limbless carnivorous reptile with a length of 6' or more, and weighing 45 pounds or more.

Raven
A black omnivorous bird with a 39-57" wingspan. Ravens are up to 26" in length and weigh 1-4 pounds.

Bat
Small winged flying vegetarian mammal who eats fruit. Weighs 2-3 pounds.

Alright, you've got the low down on our animal avatars! Pair them with their respective witchy mistresses using the clues & chart below.

The Clues

- Freya and her familiar have the same number of syllables in their names
- Eunice and Lucinda's familiars are vegetarians
- Serena and Millicent's familiars are reptiles
- Eunice, Esmerelda, Merlinda, and Lucinda's familiars are mammals
- Merlinda's familiar is smaller than Esmerelda's
- Esmerelda, Merlinda, and Millicent's familiars are wingless
- Eunice's familiar is larger than Esmerelda's familiar

	CAT	RAVEN	BAT	DRAGON	WOLF	PEGASUS	SERPENT
MILLICENT							
EUNICE							
SERENA							
FREYA							
MERLINDA							
LUCINDA							
ESMERELDA							

Complete the recipe for the love spell below. Fill in the blanks with the missing word or phrase. Then plug those words into the corresponding blanks on the next page to complete the spell. *(Note: You can do this one alone, but it's also fun to do with your familiar!)*

1. Adjective ______________________
2. Adverb ______________________
3. Adjective ______________________
4. Liquid ______________________
5. Noun ______________________
6. Adjective ______________________
7. Adjective ______________________
8. Noun ______________________
9. Noun ______________________
10. Noun ______________________
11. Adjective ______________________
12. Location ______________________
13. Adjective ______________________
14. Verb ending in ING ______________________
15. Noun ______________________
16. Verb ______________________
17. Adjective ______________________
18. Noun ______________________

THE ULTIMATE LOVE SPELL

Use this ________________________ attraction spell to make the object of your affection fall ________________________ in love with you!

To begin, you'll need to gather the following ____________ objects:

- ____________
- Three drops of ____________ extract
- A(n) ____________ candle
- The petals of a flower found in a(n) ____________ ____________

Prepare a potion combining the first two ingredients.

Next carve a(n) ______________ into the candle. Then light the candle with the flame from a(n) ________________ and allow the candle to burn as you imbibe the ______________ potion.

Place the candle in ________________ during a(n) ________________ moon, and recite the following incantation while ________________ the flower petals:

"By the power of ________________,

I call upon my beloved to ________________

and accept my ________________ affection."

Within 3 days' time the target of your spell will approach you with ____________ in their heart.

Does your vocabulary skew Stygian? Prove it by unscrambling the infernal words below!

1. UICREFL ________________

2. ENRNIS ________________

3. SHDEA ________________

4. VEIDL ________________

5. NOMDE ________________

6. ELNIARFN ________________

7. MDNADE ________________

8. RLEHWETDNOR ________________

9. MBSRENTIO ________________

10. POBETAHM ________________

11. NASTCAI ________________

12. HBAMYLPES ________________

13. WEDICK ________________

14. OURTCPR ________________

15. ELFASM ________________

STRANGE AND
UNUSUAL

One of the words in each series below is misspelled. Circle the typographically terrible option to solve the puzzle!

1. telepathy | talisman | terifying

2. entrance | enhcanted | enigmatic

3. malevolant | malicious | murderous

4. alchemy | amulet | arsonic

5. incantation | incubuus | infernal

6. paranormal | pentagram | poltergiest

7. cemetary | conspiracy | ceremony

8. sinister | sorcery | spelllbook

9. neferious | necromancy | nightmares

10. werewolf | warlock | withcraft

11. bizzare | bloodthirsty | bewitching

12. headstone | horrrifying | haunting

Practice
Self-care like a
Venus Flytrap
stay Hydrated &
Destroy Whatever Pest
invades your
Personal
space

What sort of non-human companion would you love to have as your hench-creature? Dream up your ideal familiar using the prompts below and on the opposite page!

NAME (*Give your familiar a name or nickname. Perhaps your oversized lizard goes by Fluffy or your fuzzy tarantula pal goes by Legs. Give your non-human buddy a name.*)

SPECIES (*Select a creature type; it could be a bat, a wolf, or maybe even a dragon or unicorn. The choice is yours!*)

APPEARANCE (*Describe your familiar's appearance, whether it's a 1000-eyed giant spider, a jet black panther with a mouthful of fangs, or a tentacled denizen of the deep who keeps your swampy home free of riffraff.*)

SPECIAL ABILITIES (*What special talents does your familiar bring to the table? Can they mesmerize humans or fly? Maybe they can shapeshift. Describe your creature's special abilities below.*)

WEAKNESSES *(What are your familiar's vulnerabilities? Must they avoid sunlight or getting wet? Does the sound of chewing send them into an uncontrollable rage? Describe below.)*

HABITS *(Do they sleep in a coffin or require a steady diet of bones? Do they turn red when angry? Describe your familiar's habits and idiosyncracies below.)*

LIKES & DISLIKES *(What's the fastest way to your familiar's heart? More importantly, what's the fastest way to anger them and end up in their belly? Do they love Mozart or hate the smell of children? Describe below.)*

Each of the two-sentence horror stories below and on the next page contains a hidden word, find them all! (*Example: VinCE MET ERYn outside the mausoleum, arms full of incense and candles for the altar. They were going to raise the dead!*)

1. "A book ban?!" she exclaimed. "Ban this!" She hurled a grimoire at the protesters, igniting their signs in a fiery explosion.

____

2. He would come to regret his infidelity. He had crossed her one time too many, so she sat and contemplated her revenge.

____

3. There's nowhere to hide; monsters can smell your fear from miles away. I hear them getting closer.

____

4. He asked her what she was thinking about. She waxed dreamily about joining a band one day, playing haunting music and stealing the immortal souls of her audience.

____

5. If you think true evil lain to rest will stay at rest, you've got another thing coming. Evil never truly sleeps.

____

6. The reporter asked the winged creature about its fondest memories, riveted by his mysterious interview subject. "The Middle Ages was a fun era, looking back," the infernal creature mused, "We had all manner of torture, sorcery, and mayhem at our disposal!"

____

7. She invited demons into her life her to do her bidding, but she didn't know she should never let them lock eyes with her. In the end, she paid the ultimate price.

____

8. How far can enchanted brooms take a witch? Only one way to find out!

____

Fill in the blanks below with the missing word or phrase. Then plug those words into the corresponding blanks on the next page to complete the story. (*Note: You can do this one alone, but it's also fun to do with a hobgoblin!*)

1. Adjective __________
2. Adjective __________
3. Noun __________
4. Emotional state __________
5. Noun __________
6. Noun __________
7. Adjective __________
8. Noun __________
9. Noun __________
10. Liquid __________
11. Adjective __________
12. Plural noun __________
13. Adjective __________
14. Plural noun __________
15. Verb __________
16. Plural noun __________
17. Plural noun __________
18. Adjective __________
19. Plural moun __________
20. Adjective __________

HOW I MET MY UNTIMELY END

It was a(n) __________________ stormy night when I arrived at the castle. The __________________ butler answered the door at the first ring and showed me inside. My host appeared out of nowhere, dressed head to toe in __________________, and invited me into the parlor.

I was __________________ to finally get an invitation to interview the elusive __________________. Rumors swirled that he was some sort of __________________, but I had to get to the bottom of it.

"Thank you for inviting me to your __________________ home" I said. "I've been looking forward to this interview."

My host gestured for me to sit and I took out a pen and __________________, ready to begin our conversation. Before I could ask any questions the butler returned, offering me a __________________ that appeared to be filled with __________________. I took a sip, not wanting to be __________________.

"You must not get a lot of __________________ here" I began. "This castle is so far from the city."

"I don't get many visitors," my host replied, "but the few who come here are less so visitors, and more __________________ __________________ in my abode."

The room began to __________________, and before I could ask my next question I felt myself fading. The last thing I saw was the ceiling, adorned not with __________________ or a chandelier, but countless __________________. In that moment I knew my fate would be that of every other reporter who had been curious about the __________________ castle and its __________________: missing, and never to be seen __________________ again.

No, not your wedding — that *other* big day: your funeral! Let your macabre mind run wild and design your dream dirt nap using the prompts below and on the next page.

WHAT SHOULD BE DONE WITH YOUR BODY? *(Do you hope to be cremated and have your ashes sent to space? Have your body buried next to your favorite tree? Write it below!)*

WHO IS GIVING YOUR EULOGY AND WHO WILL YOUR PALLBEARERS BE? *(Who's getting blessed — or cursed — with the honors?)*

IF YOU'RE GETTING A TOMBSTONE, WHAT SHOULD BE ETCHED INTO IT? *(See you soon? Resting in Power? You decide!)*

WHAT MUSIC SHOULD BE PLAYED? *(A New Orleans jazz band? Your favorite punk album? A famed piece of classical music? Let your loved ones know how your send-off should be soundtracked below!)*

WHAT SHOULD YOUR OBITUARY SAY? *(Jot down how you want to be memorialized below.)*

WHO OR WHAT ARE YOU GOING TO HAUNT? *(Hoping to create chaos from beyond the grave? Plan it now!)*

ADDITIONAL ITEMS ON YOUR WISH LIST *(Do you hope to be buried in your favorite pajamas or have your mourners dress in your favorite color? Add your additional requests below!)*

Math Puzzle: Creepy Calculations (Page 3)

$10 \times 10 = 100$

$100 - 10 = 90$

$90 \div 2 = 45$

$45 \div (10 \div 2) = 9$

$9 + (10 + 10) = 29$

Word Search: Parapsychology (Page 1)

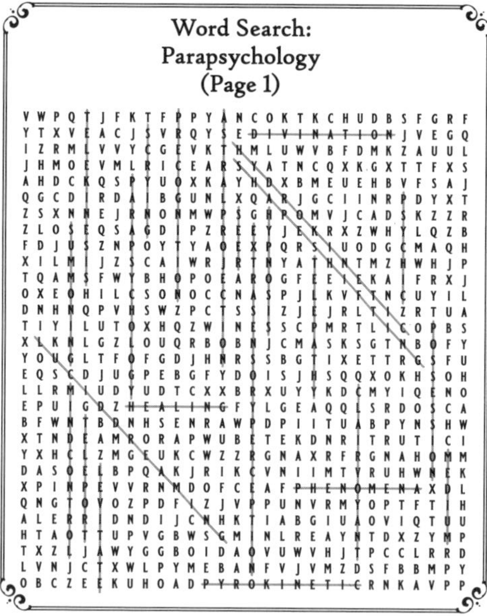

Word Jumble: Witchy Wordplay (Page 11)

1. Coven
2. Hexed
3. Cauldron
4. Broomstick
5. Grimoire
6. Warlock
7. Sorcery
8. Familiar
9. Conjure
10. Sigil
11. Curse
12. Candle
13. Charm
14. Black Magic
15. Alchemy

Crossword Puzzle: Haunted Hijinks (Pages 7 - 8)

ACROSS:

3. Sleepy Hollow
5. Banshee
7. Bloody Mary
9. Snapchat
11. Ouija
12. Alcatraz
16. Myrtle
17. Pac-Man
18. Large Marge
20. Spook
23. Sarah Winchester
25. Freddy
26. White House
27. Casper

DOWN:

1. Shirley Jackson
2. Boo Berry
4. Beetlejuice
6. Phantasm
8. Dead
10. Poltergeist
13. The Flying Dutchman
14. Dia de los Muertos
15. La Llorona
19. Overlook
20. Scrooge
21. Whaley
22. Séance
24. Ectoplasm

Spot the Difference #1 (Page 9)

Spot the Difference #2 (Page 10)

Maze: Fear The Reaper! (Page 12)

Homograph Horror (Pages 13 - 14)

1. Bat
2. Web
3. Conspiracy
4. Entrance
5. Familiar
6. Grave
7. Medium
8. Spell

Cryptogram I (Page 16)

Normalize unleashing a malevolent poltergeist on men who won't take "no" for an answer.

Quotable Creeps (Page 19)

1. *Dracula*
2. *Poltergeist*
3. *The Fly*
4. *Frankenstein*
5. *Scream*
6. *Psycho*
7. *Night of the Living Dead*
8. *The House on Haunted Hill*
9. *Nosferatu*
10. *Bride of Frankenstein*

Cryptogram II (Page 21)

No, I'm not fine, I'm a centuries old witch cut off from my rightful powers and trapped in a fragile human form.

Crossword Puzzle: Deities & Demons (Pages 23 - 24)

ACROSS:	DOWN:
4. Dybbuk	1. Kelpie
8. Asgard	2. Gorgon
9. Osiris	3. Pride
10. Mephistopheles	4. Death
12. Nyx	5. Bastet
13. Sulphur	6. Krampus
16. Lilith	7. Lovecraft
17. Jinn	11. Styx
18. Hecate	14. Leviathan
20. Baphomet	15. Wine
24. Pomegranate	19. Cerberus
26. Legion	21. Beelzebub
27. Nemesis	22. Loki
	23. Doll
	25. Goat

Logic Puzzle: Bloody Bodycount (Pages 25 - 26)

- "Bloodsucking" Bart Hart: 12
- Sal "The Slasher" Marini: 24
- "Masked" Marco Martinez: 19
- Tabitha "Stabby Tabby" Thorn: 6
- "Cannibal" Esther Goldman: 11
- "Violent" Violet Hall: 34
- "Dreaded" Donovan Grant: 17

Rhyme Time (Page 22)

1. Fat Bat
2. Pentagram Tram
3. Witch Glitch
4. Creep Heap
5. Hearse Curse
6. Ghost Host
7. Goth Sloth
8. Cool Ghoul
9. Sex Hex
10. Hell Belle

Math Puzzle: Macabre Math (Page 27)

16 + 16 + 16 = 48

0 × 4 = 0

16 ÷ 4 = 4

16 = 16

4 + 16 + 0 + 16 = 36

36 ÷ 4 = 9

Word Search: Spell It Out (Page 28)

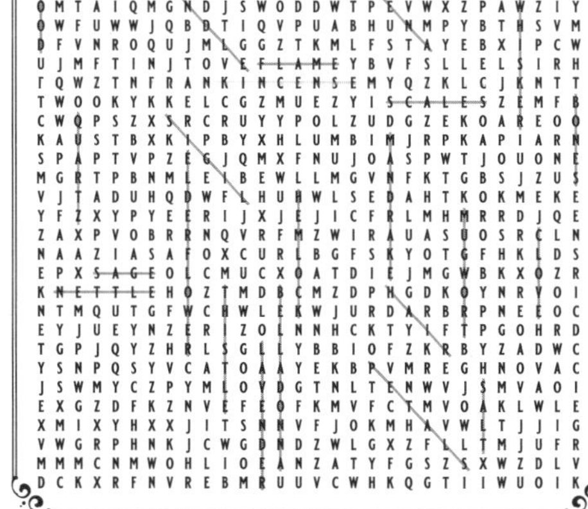

2 Truths & 1 Lie: True Crime Edition (Pages 31 - 32)

Puzzle 1: b.

Puzzle 2: c.

Puzzle 3: c.

Puzzle 4: a.

Puzzle 5: a.

Puzzle 6: c.

Puzzle 7: c.

Puzzle 8: b.

Word Search: Graveyard Games (Page 34)

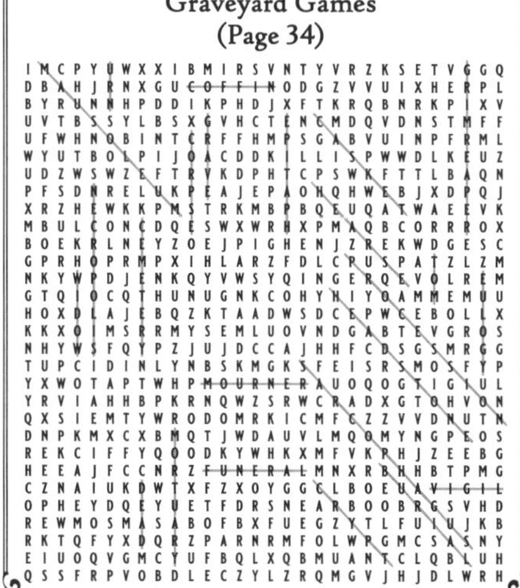

Cryptic Creatures (Page 35)

1. Zombie
2. Werewolf
3. Dracula
4. Dorian Gray
5. Frankenstein's creature
6. Mummy
7. Medusa
8. Mr. Hyde

Word Jumble: Calling All Cryptids (Page 36)

1. Loch Ness Monster
2. Mothman
3. Sasquatch
4. Chupacabra
5. Abominable Snowman
6. Jersey Devil
7. Mermaid
8. Wendigo
9. Minotaur
10. Bunyip
11. Jackalope
12. Pegasus
13. Kraken
14. Werewolf
15. Shapeshifter

Cryptogram III (Page 37)

In my next life I'm coming back as an ominous dark mist.

Rebus Puzzle: Rebus Ritual (Pages 39 - 40)

1. Ark + Cane = Arcane
2. Bee + Witch = Bewitch
3. Pen + Tag + Ram = Pentagram
4. Neck + Row + Man + Sea = Necromancy
5. Sir + M + Money = Ceremony
6. Ban + She = Banshee
7. C + Oven = Coven
8. Dive + In + Nation = Divination

Word Search: Spot The Specter (Page 43)

```
Y A I R T S P O O K Y Y F A U W Y Z B M E C U W Q F G O Q Y
P I P W F L U S K E L E T O N C T N Y Z D V T C T E K C O O
M R G Y Q E U G B M W Z B S P M X P B Z M F X Q E C G G X L
A J W U S S O D X D X Z J I R O P F R D U Z F Y T T W M L I
H O R M D O U J P T E G Y M R B L E D E T R U Q B O O K M X
X I A C C H I L L I N G V N Q N I T W A S E H N K P C I V H
N Q I A M M E P U Y M X K Z E H C H E H H E J L N L Y L K D
X A T S J F X S Q V D H R C X B D G S R Z N N D A A K M Q K
K T H O P W J B G R A V E Y A R D B C A G G L C N S E M G A
J G Y S E E Z R F S Z E I X P I E A X S G E S L E M A B C Z
T U S H F X C B L F V R L G B W Z Z D T K N I M X R G K R D
X N P P A C K T M F H W L G E C T N W R Y X H S Z G W Q E Q
V J I V Z U U P E H C O E H H Z T Q P A L V C P T D T Y E O
D X R S R T N M C R U A F K A R Y M U L S H A D O W Y J P M
A G I P E K M T U T S W M S I M P E K P X F B Z T M O B Y I
P H T O N E T W E I D L H F W B N I R L X B P H A N T O M N
P U U E B U K C P D P D E M A V T K Z A X E S N K N K G I X
A V Q C D S A D A O T L Q T E P U U F N Q M W K O K S X V Y
R F T I T N E V D I B W A D A B R W N E Q L R Y R C F O D Y
I C O Z S O Z H T I U R M N O F N M P K P W Y B S J S U P A
T Y G A R K A E M P S H B M C N E C R O M A N C Y A P S P X
I P E U S C I B S H Y T N T K H O H X I K U T X N L B J S O
O E P F E H H U A A O S U O S C E W B T P N B S O U J U V H
N R Q G A E Y T B N X T P R N U T T A G U O Q Y U O Q Q L B
F Z V H N X Q N C T D P C G B Y K O T V L O I G I K F W R Q
W I F O C J H B M A G O J E T A Z D E E O P D P J Z X G P K
Y U Y S E B D E X S W U N L M J N D Q V K A Y N A A X R P E
Y H Z T O J P X R M F L H E A K B C D O F M W J D H L K C J
J B R Z X W C X P E A R G U D L V M E U M V L W J Q K A V O
J X F P U A K U P C N N H K J I C V H F B T Y I T N J F R P
```

Secret Spell (Pages 41 - 42)

1. Arsenic
2. Cauldron
3. Alchemy
4. Cryptid
5. Haunted
6. Exorcism

Rhyming Riddles (Page 49)

1. Grave Rave
2. Chiller Killer
3. Sinister Minister
4. Beast Feast
5. Haunt Jaunt
6. Lupine Whine
7. Night Flight
8. Undead Fed
9. Lair Flair
10. Bizarre Scar

Hidden Horrors: Terrifying Tips (Pages 51 - 52)

1. Want to maintain an appearance that's youthful and exotiC? ASK ETernally beautiful creatures like vampires to reveal their secrets! (Casket)

2. Need a break from your adult responsibilities? Try getting possessed and beinG HOST to an infernal entity for a change! (Ghost)

3. With the right amount of WIT, CHarm, and scheming, anything you want can be yours! (Witch)

4. No matter what ocCURS, EDucating yourself in the Dark Arts will always be a transferable skill. (Cursed)

5. You may want to staB AT your enemies, but a hex is so much less traceable. (Bat)

6. When casting a hex on your adversary, what's viTAL IS MANaging your expectations; their downfall may not be immediate, but it will be satisfying. (Talisman)

7. If you find yourself near a siren COVE, Never allow yourself to listen to their song; next thing you know, you'll be drowning. (Coven)

8. Today is the day — take up necromancy, summon a dragon and go for a riDE! ADventure awaits! (Dead)

Crossword Puzzle: Blood Sucking
(Pages 53 - 54)

ACROSS:
2. Count Chocula
4. Baobhan Sith
7. Santa Carla
8. Renfield
12. Vlad the Impaler
14. Stake
15. Garlic
16. *Twilight*
17. Ambrogio
19. *Once Bitten*
21. Carpathian
23. *The Hunger*
24. Van Helsing
25. Buffy
27. Béla Lugosi
28. Báthory
29. Anne Rice

DOWN:
1. *Salem's Lot*
3. *Bloodletting*
5. *Nosferatu*
6. Barnabas
9. Carmilla
10. Chupacabra
11. Reflection
13. Dhampir
18. Sire
20. *The Vampyre*
22. Porphyria
23. *True Blood*
26. Coffin

Crossword Puzzle: Coven Conundrum
(Pages 61 - 62)

ACROSS:
2. Grimoire
5. Rasputin
6. Bell Witch
9. *The Craft*
12. Maleficent
17. Morgan Le Fay
18. Glinda
20. Satanic
23. Eastwick
24. Familiar
25. Blair
26. Sanderson
28. Potion

DOWN:
1. Ursula
3. Macbeth
4. Witch Hazel
7. Hex
8. Marie Laveau
10. Salem
11. Tituba
13. Willow
14. Broomstick
15. Gillian
16. Grandmama
19. Baba Yaga
21. Cauldron
22. Darrin
27. Sabrina

2 Truths & 1 Lie: Paranormal Edition
(Pages 67 - 68)

Puzzle 1: b.
Puzzle 2: c.
Puzzle 3: a.
Puzzle 4: c.
Puzzle 5: a.
Puzzle 6: b.
Puzzle 7: a.
Puzzle 8: b.

Maze: Haunted Hollow
(Page 55)

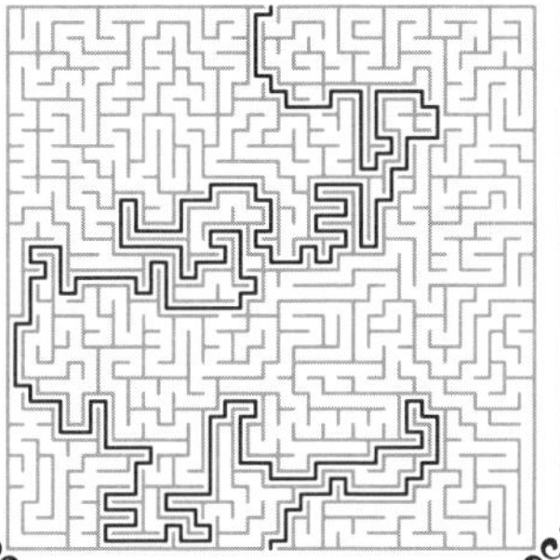

Math Puzzle: Necromancy By Numbers
(Page 63)

$11 \times 11 = 121$
$12 \times 11 = 132$
$20 - 11 = 9$
$16 - 9 = 7$
$11 \times 16 = 176$
$176 \div 11 = 16$

Word Search: Movie Monsters
(Page 64)

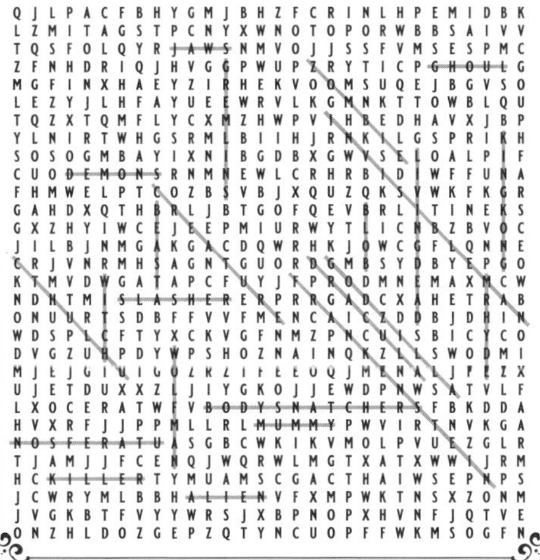

Cryptogram IV
(Page 56)

Be the horrifying retribution-obsessed demon you needed when you were younger.

Rebus Puzzle: Reaper's Rebus
(Pages 59 - 60)

1. Head + Stone = Headstone
2. Cough + Fin = Coffin
3. Frank + In + Stein = Frankenstein
4. Hem + Lock = Hemlock
5. Ink + Cube + Bus = Incubus
6. Ma + Cab = Macabre
7. Men + Ace = Menace
8. Shapes + Shift = Shapeshift

Spooky Start to Finish
(Page 65)

1. Baphomet
2. Tomb
3. Banshee
4. Enchanted
5. Divination
6. Necropolis
7. Sigil
8. Lupine
9. Enigmatic
10. Crows
11. Succubus
12. Sorcery

Logic Puzzle: Where's The Wraith?
(Pages 69 - 70)

- Agatha: Manor
- Marie: Castle
- Irving: Forest
- William: Hotel
- Sylvia: Library
- Oscar: Pub
- Anne: Lighthouse

Maze:
Saving Sasquatch
(Page 71)

Cryptogram V
(Page 72)

Good things are coming; they're called vengeance and necromancy.

Logic Puzzle:
Find The Familiar
(Pages 73 - 74)

- Serena: Dragon
- Eunice: Pegasus
- Esmerelda: Wolf
- Merlinda: Cat
- Lucinda: Bat
- Freya: Raven
- Millicent: Serpent

Word Jumble:
What The Hell?
(Page 77)

1. Lucifer
2. Sinner
3. Hades
4. Devil
5. Demon
6. Infernal
7. Damned
8. Netherworld
9. Brimstone
10. Baphomet
11. Satanic
12. Blasphemy
13. Wicked
14. Corrupt
15. Flames

Typos of Terror!
(Page 79)

1. telepathy | talisman | *terifying*
2. entrance | *enhcanted* | enigmatic
3. *malevolant* | malicious | murderous
4. alchemy | amulet | *arsonic*
5. incantation | *incubuus* | infernal
6. paranormal | pentagram | *poltergiest*
7. *cemetary* | conspiracy | ceremony
8. sinister | sorcery | *spelllbook*
9. *neferious* | necromancy | nightmares
10. werewolf | warlock | *withcraft*
11. *bizzare* | bloodthirsty | bewitching
12. headstone | *horrrifying* | haunting

Hidden Horrors: Short Story Secrets
(Pages 83 - 84)

1. "A book BAN?!" SHE Exclaimed. "Ban this!" She hurled a grimoire at the protesters, igniting their signs in a fiery explosion. (Banshee)

2. He would come to regret his infidelity. He had crossed her one time too many, so she SAT ANd contemplated her revenge. (Satan)

3. There's nowhere to hiDE; MONSters can smell your fear from miles away. I hear them getting closer. (Demons)

4. He asked her what she was thinking about. She waxed dreamily about joining A BAND ONE Day, playing haunting music and stealing the immortal souls of her audience. (Abandoned)

5. If you think true eVIL LAIN to rest will stay at rest, you've got another thing coming. Evil never truly sleeps. (Villain)

6. The reporter asked the winged creature about its fondest memories, riveted by his mysterious interview subject. "The Middle Ages was a FUN ERA, Looking back," the infernal creature mused, "We had all manner of torture, sorcery, and mayhem at our disposal!" (Funeral)

7. She invited demons into her life her to do her bidding, but she didn't know she should never let tHEM LOCK eyes with her. In the end, she paid the ultimate price. (Hemlock)

8. How fAR CAN Enchanted brooms take a witch? Only one way to find out! (Arcane)